Praise for Jehovah-Jireh

"*Jehovah-Jireh* by Mary J. Nelson is a source of hope when hope is running low. You will be encouraged as you walk with biblical characters and current-day individuals though their times of struggle and need. God was faithful then, and He is faithful today. This book will help you stay consistent in letting God lead you through difficult times. It is a book to savor. Hang out with each story, each life application and prayer. Allow yourself to marinate in the truth and the power of God's promises. . .let them take root, and you will be truly blessed."

—Kim Bushman, PhD, Licensed Psychologist,
Founder of Water's Edge Counseling & Healing Center

"Mary Nelson has done it again! *Jehovah-Jireh* speaks both to the head and the heart. . .and is a rich, biblical reminder of how much God loves and takes care of His children. Full of practical advice and spiritual insights, Mary passionately shares how our Father always provides for our needs. Sharing stories of familiar biblical characters and contemporary friends, Mary has written a book that is refreshing water for burdened and weary souls."

—Steve Hudson, CEO, Global Youth Initiative

"Mary's insightful telling of the stories of God's supernatural provision for Abraham, the prophet Elisha, for Jesus, and others from the Bible, as well as those amazing stories from believers in our time, comes alive and stirs the heart of the reader to see God as our Creator, sustainer, and provider of not just all of our needs, but of even of the deepest desires of our hearts. Mary weaves into each page an invitation to know God more intimately, to spend time with cultivating our relationship with Jesus, and to expect to hear from and receive direction from the Holy Spirit. When He directs our path in a certain way, and we don't understand, we can put our trust in Him, knowing that *'God's ways, are higher than our ways.'* One of my favorite and most impacting thoughts Mary shares is,' *'God will give you everything that you need to succeed: His wisdom, His* ʹmies, and His strength to carry out ʹeh as one of those books that will ırney."

ι Rickard,
Founders IAHM–Int   /linistries,
Founders RAIN–Resurrection Apostolic International Network

"Just as a compass always points toward true north, every story in Mary's book points to *Jehovah-Jireh: The God Who Provides*. As you read her book, it's like sitting with a dear friend—a friend who knows scripture, loves the Lord, and wants to encourage and bless you. Find a comfortable, quiet place to read and receive. The God of time and eternity will draw ever closer and provide you with peace, joy, wisdom, strength, and grace. Thank you, Mary, for this gift."

—Bill Bohline, Founding Pastor, Hosanna! Lutheran Church,
Author: *It's Sunday, but Monday's Comin'*

"The majority of you who read this book will come to know Mary Nelson as a Christ-centered, Spirit-filled, poignant, dynamic writer and storyteller. And she is. I have been privileged to also know her as a person and pastor. I can assure you she embodies and models the words on the pages of this stirring book. She knows firsthand and trusts *the God who provides*—and she is passionate about helping others do the same. If you read *Jehovah-Jireh* with an open mind and heart, you will also become one who trusts God more as a result of her anointed ministry."

—Ryan Alexander, Lead Pastor, Hosanna! Church, Lakeville, MN

"Renowned Christian Theologian J.I. Packer once said that, 'the most important thing about God is what you think of Him.' In essence, he was saying our perception of God is critical to a healthy relationship with Him. In this new book, Mary is dismantling a somewhat popular opinion in our culture that God is austere, ambivalent, and distant from the needs of humanity. Nothing could be further from the truth, and Mary convincingly demonstrates through scripture and stories that God is good and can be trusted with all of life's challenges!"

—Tim Hatt, Kingdom Expansion Pastor,
Hosanna! Church, Lakeville, MN

"While reading *Jehovah-Jireh: The God Who Provides*, I soon discovered how Mary J. Nelson has a marvelous way of making the Bible stories come alive, causing them to become relevant to our lives today. The more I read her devotions and prayers, the more I appreciate the way God speaks to my heart and meets the needs in my daily life. Mary has a way of gently reminding us that 'Only You can fill the God-hole in my heart. Only You can satisfy. You are enough.' I highly recommend this inspiring and informative book to men and women of all ages."

—Anita Corrine Donihue, Author of the When I'm
on My Knees Series and Other Inspirational Books

JEHOVAH JIREH

The God Who Provides

60 Story-Based Meditations & Prayers

MARY J. NELSON

SHILOH RUN PRESS
An Imprint of Barbour Publishing, Inc.

Print ISBN 978-1-68322-010-7

eBook Editions:
Adobe Digital Edition (.epub) 978-1-68322-303-0
Kindle and MobiPocket Edition (.prc) 978-1-68322-307-8

Published in association with the literary agency of Credo Communications, LLC, Grand Rapids, Michigan, www.credocommunications.net.

Cover Design: Greg Jackson, Thinkpen Design

Published by Shiloh Run Press, an imprint of Barbour Publishing, Inc., P.O. Box 719, Uhrichsville, Ohio 44683, www.shilohrunpress.com

Our mission is to publish and distribute inspirational products offering exceptional value and biblical encouragement to the masses.

Member of the
Evangelical Christian
Publishers Association

Dedication

To my parents, Ray and Jeanne Hangge,
for a lifetime of love, support, and prayers.
Thank you for everything. I love you.

Acknowledgments

Jehovah-Jireh: The God Who Provides is the second in a series on the names of God. The revelation contained in these pages came from seeking God's heart through the good times and the not so good times, and through years of ministry with people struggling to have their physical, emotional, spiritual, and financial needs met. For making this book a reality, my deepest gratitude goes to:

Jehovah-Jireh: for providing everything I truly need. You are enough.

My husband, Howie: for forty years, you have been a hard worker and a faithful provider; I couldn't do this ministry without your love and sacrifice.

My children and grandchildren—Bryan, Kelly, Sharmi, Xavier, and Lila: my heart overflows with gratefulness for the beautiful family God has provided; we are blessed beyond measure.

Hosanna! prayer, Pray for the Cure, Healing Prayer, and prayer team 3: for the honor and privilege of ministering alongside you. Your passion and heart to see people receive all that Jesus died for humbles and inspires me.

My small groups, up north gang, and high school friends: your loyalty and trustworthiness is a priceless gift and a timeless reminder of God's provision.

Everyone whose personal quest for provision gave me the inspiration for the testimonies in this book: may your stories bring hope and encouragement to others in need and remind them to seek first His Kingdom.

My agents Ann Byle and Tim Beals of Credo Communications: for partnering with me to help bring God's promise of provision into the lives of those who need it most.

Kelly McIntosh, Shalyn Sattler, and the entire Barbour Publishing family: for using your amazing creative talents and wisdom to glorify Jehovah-Jireh, the God who provides.

Finally, to my readers: your kindness and encouragement keeps me writing. Someday, I will meet you all in heaven and thank you face-to-face.

Contents

Before You Begin

And now that you belong to Christ, you are the true children of Abraham.
You are his heirs, and God's promise to Abraham belongs to you.
GALATIANS 3:29

MOUNT MORIAH IN JERUSALEM (SALEM), 2054 BC

"[Abraham!] Take your son, your only son—yes, Isaac, whom you love so much—and go to the land of Moriah. Go and sacrifice him as a burnt offering on one of the mountains, which I will show you" (Genesis 22:2). *What? But God!* Had he heard correctly? How could this be? This promised son whom he had waited for twenty-five years to be born—the same son through whom his descendants would outnumber the stars in the sky—this miracle child his wife Sarah had birthed and nursed at her breast at the ripe old age of ninety-one—he was to sacrifice *this* son as a burnt offering?

Sighing deeply, he remembered twenty-five years ago when God told him to leave the comforts of his home and travel across the desert to an unknown land. He was obedient because he believed in God and he believed He would do what He promised. Years passed, not without hardship, not without doubts, and not without misguided human efforts to speed up God's promise. Finally, when he was one hundred years old, Isaac was born. Oh, how he loved the boy! Surely, God would not take away his only son. God had promised to make him the father of a multitude of nations and to extend their everlasting covenant to all his offspring from generation to generation. How could this happen without Isaac? It made no sense. But he had learned that God's commands usually defied human logic. Even so, he believed. God had always been faithful to him. Yes, he heard correctly. He knew God, and he knew His voice. Again, he must obey. Clearly, God had a plan and a purpose in making this outrageous request.

He got up early the next morning, saddled his donkey, and set out for the long journey from Beersheba to the land of Moriah with two of his servants and his son. Before leaving, he chopped wood for a fire for a burnt offering. They traveled most of the way through the rugged terrain in silence, he in deep thought and clearly troubled. *I don't understand, God. I waited all these years for this son You promised. I have been faithful to Your commands. All for this?*

On the third day of their journey, he looked up and saw Mount Moriah at a distance. He knew this was the place. "Stay here with the donkey," he told the servants. "The boy and I will travel a little farther. We will worship there, and then we will come right back." *Oh God, surely we will return together!* Then he placed the wood for the burnt offering on Isaac's shoulders, while he carried the coals for making the fire along with the knife. He thought ruefully about the knife he had used many times to kill sheep for the sacrifice. *I am to use this same knife to kill my own son? But God!*

As the two of them walked together, the boy asked, "Father?" "Yes, my son?" he replied. "We have the fire and the wood," Isaac said, "but where is the sheep for the burnt offering?" Looking into Isaac's troubled face, he replied, "God will provide a sheep for the burnt offering, my son." *Surely God, You will!* They walked on together in silence, Isaac pondering his father's answer, and Abraham growing more agitated as they came closer to the place God had told him to go.

When they arrived, Abraham busied himself by building an altar and arranging the wood. When all was ready and he could stall no more, he looked at his son. It was time. Wide-eyed and motionless, Isaac stood staring at him as Abraham began to bind the boy with rope. Curiously, Isaac didn't object, even when he laid him on the altar on top of the wood. Gazing into his son's eyes, Abraham saw an odd combination of confusion and childlike trust, the look of a son who trusts his father even when he doesn't understand the circumstances. When Abraham could no longer bear it, he turned his eyes away, picked up the knife, and lifted it over Isaac's head. At the very moment he was about to lower it, a voice called out to him from heaven: "Abraham! Abraham!" "Yes," he replied eagerly. "Here I am!" "Don't lay a hand on the boy!" the voice said. "Do not hurt him in any way, for now I know that you truly fear God. You have not withheld from Me even your son, your only son."

His knees buckling, he stumbled back from the altar as a myriad of emotions flooded his heart. *Oh God, oh my God!* Just then, he looked up and saw a ram caught by its horns in a thicket. *The sacrifice!* Untying and releasing his precious son from the altar, he took the ram and sacrificed it as a burnt offering in his place. He named the place *Jehovah-Jireh*, meaning "the LORD will provide."

Before leaving the mountain, the voice called out to him once more: "Because you have obeyed Me and have not withheld even your son, your only son, I swear by My own name that I will certainly bless you. I will multiply your descendants beyond number, like the stars in the sky and the sand on the seashore. Your descendants will conquer the cities of their enemies. And through your descendants all the nations of the earth will be blessed—all because you have obeyed Me." Making their way down the mountain, Abraham was filled with wonder at the faithfulness of God and what had just happened.

Indeed, on the mountain of the Lord, it will be provided. (Based on Genesis 22:1–19.)

Four thousand years ago, Abraham faced severe testing and seemingly insurmountable circumstances and probably the greatest test of faith in human history. But his obedience opened the door for God's provision for all who put their faith in Him (Galatians 3:7). At a time when the people were required to offer animal sacrifices to atone for their sins under ancient Levitical law, he had the faith to offer his own son as a sacrifice even though God had told him Isaac would be the son through whom his descendants would be counted. Now, by this stage in his life, Abraham had a long history with God. He had learned many difficult lessons about obedience and God's faithfulness. He reasoned that if Isaac died, God was able to bring him back to life again (Hebrews 11:17–19). God only wanted Abraham to sacrifice Isaac in his heart, making it clear that he indeed loved Him above all else.

And because he withheld nothing from God, Abraham found that God returned more than he could have ever dreamed. He not only gave Abraham an entire nation of descendants through Isaac, but He promised this nation would be blessed wherever they went and in whatever they did. They would have victory over their enemies, abundant prosperity, and blessing over their lands and their work. He would care for their every need at the proper time and promised that the entire world would stand in awe of the blessings He would pour on them. All He required was devotion to the one true God and obedience to His ways (Deuteronomy 28:1–13).

Two thousand years later, on the same mountain God provided a ram for Abraham to sacrifice in place of his son, the Father offered up His own Son as a sacrifice for us all. On the mountain of the Lord, He provided the solution for our sin problem forever. As followers of Jesus, we have been grafted into Abraham's family tree and receive the same blessings God promised him (Romans 11:17). We are God's children, and everything He has belongs to us (Galatians 4:7)! He will certainly supply all your needs from His glorious riches, which have been given to us in Christ Jesus (Philippians 4:19). He is Jehovah-Jireh, the God who provides (Genesis 22:14). When you put Him above everything else—even when it makes no sense, or it means giving up something you want or doing something you don't want to do—He will surely give you everything you need and then some.

In this book you will find compelling teaching on promises of provision in the scriptures, prayers for seeking God to meet your every need, and powerful Kingdom stories that will encourage you to trust in God alone as your provider. Whatever need you may be facing today, my hope is that you withhold nothing from your God and come to desire Him more than any blessing you receive from His hand. I pray that His love will overwhelm you and He will always be enough to fill your lack. Because you belong to Christ and you are a true child of Abraham, all of God's promises to him belong to you. May He bless you wherever you go and in whatever you do, and return more than you could ever dream. On the mountain of the Lord, in that deep place of intimacy, may you receive everything you need from the God who provides.

The God of Abundance

I will bless her with abundant provisions;
her poor I will satisfy with food.
PSALM 132:15 NIV

Sighing heavily, she closed the door. The merciless debt collector had delivered the final blow. Tears pooling in her eyes, she longed for her dear husband, a man of God and one of Elisha's prophets. He loved the Lord and served Him so faithfully! And then he died, leaving her with a mountain of debt and ruthless creditors like this one beating at her door. Her sons had been her only hope against a future of begging on the streets. And now this creditor wanted to take them away, too. *I must find Elisha,* she thought as she gathered herself and hurried out the door to the place where the Lord's prophets gathered. When she found him, she dropped to her knees and cried out, "My husband who served you is dead, and you know how he feared the LORD. But now a creditor has come, threatening to take my two sons as slaves."

"What can I do to help you?" Elisha asked calmly. Just as hope began to well up within her, he asked another question. "Tell me, what do you have in the house?" Thinking of her bare shelves and everything else she was forced to sell to keep the creditors at bay, she responded forlornly, "Nothing at all, except a flask of olive oil." The seriousness of her predicament overwhelmed her all over again. *And how can one paltry flask of olive oil possibly make a dent in the insurmountable debt I must pay off to keep my sons? It would never satisfy the creditor, and I'd be foolish to think it would.* But Elisha was clearly undaunted.

"Borrow as many empty jars as you can from your friends and neighbors," he ordered. "Then go into your house with your sons and shut the door behind you. Pour olive oil from your flask into the jars, setting each one aside when it is filled."

Set each one aside when it is filled? My flask will fill more than one? She didn't understand, but she quickly moved into action. The Lord had spoken through His prophet and, when the Lord spoke, she listened. She did exactly as she was told. She sent her sons out to borrow as many empty jars as they could find from all their friends and neighbors. When they had finished gathering the jars, she shut the door behind them and filled the first jar to the brim. Marveling that there was still plenty of olive oil in the flask, she filled the second. And the third. *Still oil in the flask?* Amazed, she filled the next one and the next. Her sons kept bringing the borrowed jars to her, and she filled each one full to the brim! "Bring me another jar," she said with excitement to one of her sons. "There aren't any more!" he told her. And at that moment, the olive oil stopped flowing.

Standing back in wonder, she looked at her flask of olive oil and the rows of jars lining the walls of her home that were now filled to the brim with oil. *I must tell Elisha!* She ran to the place the prophets gathered and told the man of God what had happened. Nodding and smiling, he said to her, "Now sell the olive oil and pay your debts, and you and your sons can live on what is left over." (Based on 2 Kings 4:1–7.)

In Old Testament times, the law allowed people to sell themselves or a loved one into slavery to pay their debts. But the law also commanded creditors to show mercy to people facing extreme circumstances. While the creditor extended no mercy to this woman, Elisha showed her that God's compassion was greater than both the law and her dire situation. Even though Elisha's instructions made no logical sense to her, she took the only thing she had left—a simple flask of oil used for cooking, fuel, and lamps—and did exactly what she was told. She humbled herself and reached out for help from her neighbors and friends. Then she shut the door behind her to be alone with the Lord and watch His miracle unfold. God rewarded her faithfulness and her willingness to obey. The oil flowed freely from the flask as long as there were enough jars to hold it.

God never runs out of blessing, but how often do we run out of the faithfulness to receive? Beloved, like this widow, you may have desperate needs today. Be faithful and obey, even when it makes no sense. Keep bringing Him your empty jars and watch His blessings overflow. He is indeed a God of abundance.

Prayer

Lord, thank You for the promise that You will bless me with provision and satisfy my practical needs! When I am tempted to doubt Your ability to provide, remind me of this widow and her bare shelves. Lord, You didn't run out of oil; she ran out of jars! Your provision was as much as her faith and her willingness to obey. Help me not to limit Your blessing by my lack of faith and obedience. Lord, You know all my needs today. I bring you my empty jars! Fill them to overflowing with Your unlimited oil of provision!

But Lord, in spite of my need, You are far better than all the practical blessings that come from that flask of oil. Only You can satisfy the deepest longings of my heart. Thank You for always offering free refills when I humble myself in the stillness of Your presence. I am empty, Lord. My soul thirsts for You alone. Fill me with Your Spirit, Lord. You are all I need.

Are You Here with Me or Not?

*Moses named the place Massah (which means "test") and Meribah
(which means "arguing") because the people of Israel argued with Moses
and tested the LORD by saying, "Is the LORD here with us or not?"*
EXODUS 17:7

He went from being the son of a princess to a sheep herder in
the desert until God called him from a burning bush to rescue
His people from bondage. For four hundred years, the Israelites
had lived in Egypt under Pharaoh's rule until their numbers
had grown two million strong. Now, *he* was God's chosen one
to lead this mass of humanity to their Promised Land. He
had argued with God, but to no avail. *Yes, for some reason, He
chose me.* At God's direction, he had confronted Pharaoh, until
finally, through a series of deadly plagues and broken promises,
Pharaoh finally relented. But even though God had shown them
His love and His power many times over, these wretched people
complained incessantly! How could they possibly long for the
days in Egypt where their slave masters whipped them into
submission and worked them to near death?

He could understand the first time they complained.
After releasing them, Pharoah quickly changed his mind and
mobilized all the forces in Egypt to chase them down. Trapped
between the mountains and the Red Sea with Pharaoh's army
in hot pursuit, they forgot how the Lord's mighty power had
rescued them from their captors. "Why did you bring us out
here to die in the wilderness?" they lamented. "Weren't there
enough graves for us in Egypt? What have you done to us? Why
did you make us leave Egypt? It's better to be a slave in Egypt
than a corpse in the wilderness!" But he encouraged them. "Don't

be afraid. Just stand still and watch the LORD rescue you today. The Egyptians you see today will never be seen again. The LORD Himself will fight for you. Just stay calm." And the Lord did. He opened up a dry path through the sea and destroyed the entire army of Pharaoh in the process.

In spite of witnessing this incredible miracle, their incessant grumbling continued. They complained when Moses led them away from the Red Sea into the desert and the water was bitter. Again, he cried out to God on their behalf and God made the water good for them to drink. As he led them farther into the desert, they complained of no food. "If only the LORD had killed us back in Egypt," they moaned. "There we sat around pots filled with meat and ate all the bread we wanted. But now you have brought us into this wilderness to starve us all to death." But again the Lord provided. In the evening, He sent quail for meat and every morning, bread from heaven covered the ground. Each family would gather their allotted amount of this strange white substance, grind it like grain, and make it into honey cakes.

Yes, God had been a faithful provider to this community of two million as they moved from place to place to reach their promised destination. And now, they were complaining again? This time, there was no water at Rephidim, the place where they were camped. "Give us water to drink!" they demanded. Moses reached his limit. "Quiet! Why are you complaining against me? And why are you testing the LORD?" But tormented by thirst, they continued to argue. "Why did you bring us out of Egypt? Are you trying to kill us, our children, and our livestock with thirst?" Frustrated by their lack of faith, he cried out desperately to the Lord, "What should I do with these people? They are ready to stone me!"

Again, the Lord provided. "Walk out in front of the people.

Take your staff. . .and call some of the elders of Israel to join you," He instructed. "I will stand before you on the rock at Mount Sinai. Strike the rock, and water will come gushing out. Then the people will be able to drink." Again Moses did as he was told. With the elders looking on, he struck the rock with his staff and, just as the Lord had promised, water gushed out for the people to drink. *Will these people ever learn? Don't they know by now that God is with us and He will provide?* He named the place *Massah* (which means "test") and *Meribah* (which means "arguing") because the people of Israel argued with him and tested the LORD by saying, "Is the LORD here with us or not?" (Based on Exodus 14; 15:22–27; 16; 17:1–7.)

God heard the cries of His people for deliverance from their harsh Egyptian slave drivers. He knew of their suffering and came to rescue them and lead them into a land of their own, flowing with milk and honey. He provided a leader, a plan, and a promise to be with them through the entire journey and meet their every need (Exodus 3). Time after time, He made good on His promises. But every time they encountered danger, a shortage of some kind, or an inconvenience, they doubted He would provide *this* time. Instead of turning to God who had faithfully orchestrated a plan for their freedom, they grumbled, complained, and even yearned for their old familiar chains of bondage.

How often do we do the same thing? Our dire circumstances can lead to stress, fear, or even panic, and complaining to God or anyone who will listen becomes our natural response. We demand to know, as they did, is the Lord here with us or not? For them as well as us, the real problem is not the current thing we lack; it is often our lack of trust in God. When you are tempted to choose complaining and doubting, rather than praying and trusting, remember all the times God has been faithful in your journey through life and all the ways He has provided for you. Remember the times you felt trapped and He parted the sea, the times He made a way when you could see no way around your circumstances. Can He meet your needs *this* time? Turn to Him again; let Him show you He is with you!

Prayer

Lord, there are times when my circumstances overwhelm me. My needs are great and I see no way out of the mess I find myself in. Thank You, Lord, for hearing my cries for help! I know You promise to provide for my every need. Forgive me when I forget all the ways You care for me every single day! Thank You for a roof over my head; for food on the table; for family, friends, employers, and others You have put in my path to love and care for me. Forgive my ungratefulness! I'm so sorry for grumbling and complaining and making my case to everyone but You. Thank You, Lord, for Your faithfulness!

Lord, help me to focus my eyes on You and trust in Your provision, even when I don't understand Your ways. Thank You for grace and for redeeming my past mistakes. Remind me that when my circumstances seem impossible, nothing is impossible for You; even if I can't be certain about my next paycheck or my next meal, I can always be certain of You! If You can part the sea, provide bread from heaven, and make water gush from a rock to sustain two million people in the wilderness, You can provide for me! Today, I bring my needs before You, Lord. May I never again wonder whether You are with me or not!

His Very Best

*This miraculous sign at Cana in Galilee was the first time
Jesus revealed his glory. And his disciples believed in him.*
JOHN 2:11

Her eyes panned the large crowd gathered to celebrate the marriage of one of the townspeople. Her son and His disciples were invited to the celebration along with the whole village of Cana. She thought about all the food and drink necessary to host a crowd of this size for the customary week-long celebration. So much had been consumed already. And this was only the third day! *Will there ever be enough?*

It wasn't long before her concerns were validated. When she realized the wine supply had run out, she hurried to find her son. It would be considered inhospitable for the host to run out of wine. *Where would they find enough wine at this hour to spare the host such humiliation?* She spotted her son enjoying the company of some of the guests. As she approached Him, she beckoned Him to the side and said in a hushed tone, "They have no more wine."

"Dear woman, that's not our problem," He replied. "My time has not yet come." She looked intently into the eyes of the son whom she had miraculously conceived over thirty years ago; this same son who held the salvation of the entire world in His hands, whose destiny she had treasured in her heart for so many years. Certainly a little wine shortage was not beyond His power to accommodate the pressing need of this family. But they both knew if He solved this problem, His ministry would be officially launched. His identity would be exposed for all to see, and His destiny would begin to unfold. There would be no stopping it. Yes, there was no need for words. She turned to the servants standing nearby and, nodding toward her son, she said, "Do whatever He tells you."

The servants looked over at Him, awaiting their instructions. Still looking at His mother, His eyes slowly turned toward six stone water jars that were lined up against a nearby wall. The jars were used for Jewish ceremonial washing and each could hold twenty to thirty gallons. *That should be enough.* "Fill the jars with water," He told the servants. Immediately, they dispersed to find the containers they needed to carry out their assignment. After several trips back and forth from the well, the jars were filled to the brim with water. Then He told them, "Now dip some out, and take it to the master of ceremonies." So again, the servants followed His instructions.

Holding the ladle in his hand, the master of ceremonies raised it to his lips and tasted, not knowing where the wine had come from. Mary watched for his reaction, confident he would be pleased. "Come," he gestured to the bridegroom, calling him to his side. Putting his arm around the bridegroom's shoulder, he said in a loud voice for all the guests to hear, "A host always serves the best wine first. Then, when everyone has had a lot to drink, he brings out the less expensive wine. But you have kept the best until now!"

Satisfied, she looked over at her son. This miraculous sign at Cana was the first time He revealed His glory, and His disciples believed in Him. But it certainly wouldn't be the last. She would be blessed to spend a few more days with this son who changed water into wine. And then He would go out and change the world. (Based on John 2:1–12.)

It may seem odd that Jesus would choose a wedding feast to reveal His glory and perform His first miracle, and even more strange that His mother's encouragement compelled Him to do it. Perhaps He wanted to make sure she was ready for all that would come to pass. By mingling with these wedding guests and providing them with more wine, Jesus showed He wasn't dull, boring, or opposed to enjoying life. On the contrary, He came to be with the people, celebrate in their festivities, and share in their joy. His disciples believed when they witnessed this first miracle, and He used this event as a foundation for how He would do ministry moving forward.

This miracle, like the countless others He would perform, demonstrated the power and authority we have in Christ. Prepared through the scriptures, intimacy with His Father, and empowered by the Spirit, He would go on to help those in need and restore a fallen world. By changing water to wine in the same jars used for ceremonial hand washing, He symbolically replaced the purification ritual the people followed to wash away the unholy influences of the day with the spotless blood of the Lamb that would wash away the sins of the entire world. Cleansed and transformed, His followers would go into the world with the same mission—to help the needy, restore the broken, and advance the Kingdom of God.

Jesus had compassion for this bridegroom, and He has compassion for you. Your needs today may seem no greater than a lack of wine at a wedding feast, but if it matters to you, it matters to Him. You have access to the same resources He did. You have His Word, His death and resurrection gave you direct access to His Father, and His Spirit dwells within you!

Surrender your life to Him and He will not only meet your every need, He will give you His very best and more.

Prayer

Lord, when I look at others who are worse off than I am, I have often wondered if my needs aren't important enough to bring to Your attention. Thank You for reminding me that You are a God of abundance, and You care about all the details of my life. If it matters to me, it matters to You! Nothing is too insignificant to bring before Your throne of grace. You are a good and generous God!

Lord, thank You for the gift of Your Word, the power of Your presence, and Your promise to provide for all my needs. Fill me with Your Spirit, Lord. Fill me to the brim! Help me to surrender all that I have and all that I am to You. Lord, You know my needs before I ask. I trust You will provide for me. I trust You will give me Your very best and then some! Help me to walk in Your footsteps and become the world-changer You created me to be. Help me bless others through the overflow of Your presence! To You be the glory!

Always Enough

*For no matter how much they used, there was always plenty left
in the containers, just as the Lord had promised through Elijah!*
1 KINGS 17:16 TLB

Elijah was the first in a long line of prophets God would send
to rescue the people from their moral and spiritual decline. It
was a difficult and dangerous assignment, and it would grow
more so as time passed. He was obedient and brave when the
Lord sent him to confront King Ahab, one of the many wicked
and unfaithful kings who led the people astray. "As surely as the
Lord, the God of Israel, lives—the God I serve—there will be
no dew or rain during the next few years until I give the word!"
he warned the king. But Ahab only scoffed. His army was strong,
and he worshipped Baal, the god of the rain and harvest. Surely,
his priests would save them from this threat.

In the meantime, the Lord told Elijah to go east and hide
by Kerith Brook, near where it enters the Jordan River. "Drink
from the brook and eat what the ravens bring you, for I have
commanded them to bring you food," He instructed. The prophet
obeyed, and sure enough, the ravens brought him bread and meat
each morning and evening, and he drank from the brook. He was
lonely, but his needs were met. But after a while the brook dried
up, for there was no rainfall anywhere in the land. *Lord, I have been
obedient to You. I have survived on food from unclean birds, and now
there is no water!* But the Lord hadn't forgotten His prophet or His
assignment. "Go and live in the village of Zarephath, near the city
of Sidon," He said. "I have instructed a widow there to feed you."
Relieved and encouraged by the Lord's promise of sustenance, he
headed for Zarephath.

When he arrived at the gates of the village, he saw a widow gathering sticks and asked her, "Would you please bring me a little water in a cup?" As she left to get water, he realized how hungry he was and called out to her, "Bring me a bite of bread, too." She turned and lowered her head. "I swear by the Lord your God that I don't have a single piece of bread in the house," she said forlornly. "And I have only a handful of flour left and a little cooking oil in the bottom of the jar. I was just gathering a few sticks to cook this last meal, and then my son and I will die." As he pondered her words, the Lord again spoke to his spirit: "There will always be flour and olive oil left in her containers until the time when I send rain and the crops grow again!"

"Don't be afraid!" Elijah encouraged. "Go ahead and do just what you've said, but make a little bread for me first. Then use what's left to prepare a meal for yourself and your son." When he told her what the Lord had promised, she scurried off and did just as he said, and she, the prophet, and her family continued to eat for many days. There was always enough flour and olive oil left in the containers, just as the Lord had promised. (Based on 1 Kings 17:1–16.)

God provided for the prophet Elijah and this widow during a time of severe drought, but His provision came in unexpected ways. He sent bread and meat to Elijah through unclean birds, and when this provision ran out, God sent him to a widow who had nothing to give. The widow focused on all she lacked, until the prophet spoke God's truth into her seemingly dire circumstances. Their miracle of provision started with her simple act of obedience. When she stepped out in faith and prepared the "last meal," God's promise to provide came to pass. Later, this widow's son would die, but Elijah cried out to God on behalf of this widow who had opened her home to him. Without a son to provide for her, she faced a future of poverty and begging, but God answered Elijah's prayers and raised the child back to life (1 Kings 17:17–23).

At times, your situation may seem as hopeless as this widow's. You may want to use up what little you have left, throw in the towel, and be done with it. At times like this, remember that God has a plan and purpose for your life, just as He had for Elijah and this widow. He sustained them, and He will sustain you (Colossians 1:16–17). He may not speak to you through a prophet, but His Spirit lives in you and speaks to your spirit. Tell Him what you need, and obey when you hear His voice. The answer may not come in the way you expect, but it *will* come. Even after your breakthrough, your troubles may not be over. The passing of the widow's son was just one more opportunity for her to trust in the Creator to sustain His creation. The Provider knows your every need. From this day to the next, there will always be enough.

Prayer

Lord, some days I feel helpless and hopeless. Like this widow, sometimes I am tempted to throw in what little I have left and be done with the struggle. Yes, Lord, there is a severe drought in my land and I am desperate for rain. I need a fresh outpouring of Your supernatural provision! Please forgive me when I have trusted and depended on any source other than You for the needs I have right now.

Lord, today I need to hear Your voice. I sit quietly in Your presence. Holy Spirit, speak to me and tell me what to do! Lead me to the right scripture and put godly people in my path that will speak Your truth to me. Give me faith to obey Your Word even when it makes no sense and my circumstances seem impossible. Help me to believe in Your promises even when I don't understand Your ways. Lord, I'm grateful that I am Your creation and You promise to sustain Your creation. You know my needs today, Lord, and You promise to provide. Thank You that in and through You, my supply never runs out. There will always be enough.

And Then Some

After everyone was full, Jesus told his disciples, "Now gather the leftovers, so that nothing is wasted." So they picked up the pieces and filled twelve baskets with scraps left by the people who had eaten from the five barley loaves.

JOHN 6:12–13

John the Baptist was dead, beheaded as a sordid prize for a young girl whose dancing pleased the king. As soon as they told Him the devastating news, Jesus wanted to get away from the crowds and rest. They left by boat, crossing over to the far side of the Sea of Galilee to a remote area where He could be alone to grieve and pray. But people heard where Jesus was headed and followed on foot from many towns because they knew how He had healed the sick and performed many miracles. When Jesus stepped off the boat and saw the huge crowd, He felt deep compassion for them. Instead of retreating to the hills to rest and be alone, He taught them about the Kingdom and healed all who were sick.

One disciple began to grow uneasy as he watched Jesus teach and minister to this huge crowd of fifteen thousand. He knew this area well. The nearest town, his hometown of Bethsaida, was nine miles away. *These people will be hungry and need to eat soon.* After conferring with the rest of the disciples, he and the others came to Jesus with a plan. "This is a remote place, and it's already getting late," they advised. "Send the crowds away so they can go to the villages and buy food for themselves."

Jesus' answer made no sense at all. "That isn't necessary—*you* feed them." *Us? Feed them?* Seeing the incredulous looks on all the disciples' faces, Jesus turned to Philip and asked, "Philip, where can we buy bread to feed all these people?" *Is this a test? What is He thinking? No, it's impossible. Even if we could go buy enough food in Bethsaida and the surrounding villages and bring it all back here, it would take a small fortune, two hundred days' wages.* He found his voice and replied, "Even if we worked for months, we wouldn't have enough money to feed them!"

"How much bread do you have?" Jesus asked. "Go and find out." The disciples quickly dispersed to assess their food supply and soon returned with a grim report. "There's a young boy here with five barley loaves and two fish. But what good is that with this huge crowd?" asked Andrew, Simon Peter's brother. "Bring them here," Jesus said. "And tell everyone to sit down in groups of fifty to one hundred." So they all sat down on the grassy slopes in groups as Jesus directed. He took the five loaves and two fish, looked up toward heaven, gave thanks to God, and blessed them. Breaking the loaves into pieces, He gave the bread to the disciples and told them to distribute the food to the people.

Jesus' words echoed in Philip's spirit. *YOU feed them.* He marveled as he and the other disciples carried the bread to the hungry men, women, and children seated in each group. Each time they went back for more, there was plenty left to distribute. Afterward Jesus did the same with the fish. When everyone was full and had eaten as much as they wanted, He told His disciples, "Now gather the leftovers, so that nothing is wasted." So they picked up the pieces and filled twelve baskets with scraps left by the people who had eaten from the five barley loaves. Philip pondered the miracle he had just witnessed along with the rest of the crowd. *Who can feed fifteen thousand people from five barley loaves and two fishes? Surely, He is the King we have been expecting!* But Jesus had already slipped quietly away into the hills to be alone. (Based on Matthew 14:13–21; Mark 6:30–44; Luke 9:10–17; and John 6:1–15.)

The disciples took one look at the insurmountable problem before them and forgot all the previous miracles they had already witnessed through Jesus. They still didn't understand that He could provide for them, whatever need they faced. The impossible, overwhelming situation kept them from believing and from remembering who He was. Philip, a local boy from Bethsaida, got practical and immediately assessed the costs. He evaluated the problem from an earthly perspective and quickly concluded it was impossible to solve. He knew where to get food, and he knew the amount they needed would cost a small fortune. Even if they had the money, the logistics of purchasing and distributing the food to all these people by nightfall was out of the question. But Jesus challenged him. He knew full well there was no human solution that could completely address their need. So He started by asking them what they *did* have.

But instead of focusing on what they had, Andrew focused on what they lacked. He couldn't see how a boy's meager lunch could possibly make any difference. *Here's what we have, but what good is it?* But Jesus took what the young boy had and multiplied it, not just enough for fifteen thousand people, but enough to fill twelve more baskets. The disciples went from the incredulous—"You expect *us* to feed them?"—to being *part* of delivering a miracle. As they distributed the food to each hungry group, they had to depend on Jesus to keep the food coming.

What miracle do you need today? Are you telling Jesus how big your problem is, or are you telling your problem how big your Jesus is? The disciples let the sheer magnitude of the problem blind them to His power. Remember, what is impossible for man is always possible for God (Luke 18:27)! Resist the temptation to limit Him because the solution to your dilemma appears to be out of the realm of possibility. He can provide resources that are not available in the natural realm.

If you give up and offer Him nothing, God has nothing to use. But if you give Him what you *do* have—whether time, money, or talents—He can multiply what you give Him, no matter how insignificant your gift. If He can use a boy's lunch to feed the masses, He can turn your meager contribution into something great, not only to solve your own problems, but the problems of others. You might even get to be part of a miracle. Beloved, raise your expectations. He can provide for you and then some.

Prayer

Lord, You are the provider, and those who seek You lack no good thing (Psalm 34:10). Forgive me when I forget who You are and Your power to do the impossible. I'm sorry for assuming the solution to my problems rests on human shoulders alone. Help me to see the situation I face today through Your eyes of possibility instead of my own eyes of lack and limitation. Raise my expectations, Lord!

Please show me my "boy's lunch" and help me to offer it up to You with a grateful and expectant heart. Help me to trust that You can take my meager offering and use it to make a difference in my life and in the lives of others. Lord, I speak to my problem today, and I say my Jesus is bigger! I expect to see Your power and Your provision manifest in my life, and then some. Use what I give You today and let it be part of a miracle!

Jehovah Jireh: Jeff's Story

You're too old. They didn't say it that way, but Jeff knew exactly what they meant. Comments like "I bet a thirty-year-old got that job," or "Finding a job isn't easy for people our age," rolled off their tongues as if it were the gospel truth. Sometimes they tried to help: "I heard they're hiring retirees to drive for the bus company," or "Hey Jeff, Sam's Club needs part-time food demonstrators. It's a great job for retirees." Only he *wasn't* retired. He wasn't a food taster or a bus driver. He was an experienced, college-educated business developer. He was also sixty-two. A *young* sixty-two. Yes, he could probably retire early and move on to the next chapter in his life. He could probably get by financially. But God knew he wasn't ready. He enjoyed work, and he knew he had more to contribute to the marketplace. He had a new revelation of God's faithfulness, and he was excited about the next thing God had planned for him. After all these years, he had experience and wisdom that would greatly benefit any employer in his field. He wanted to retire when *he* was ready, when *God* was ready to release him into his next assignment, not the world. He wanted to finish well.

The last three years had shaken his faith to the core. Shortly after his sixtieth birthday, his employer eliminated his position. He was forced to pursue a lawsuit, endure lies about his character, and argue distorted facts used against him. During the same time, his mother passed away. To top things off, the new job he started was not turning out to be at all what the employer had promised. The company was fraught with leadership dysfunction, unclear vision, and constantly changing goals. He was tasked with achieving impossible, unrealistic results selling an overpriced service with no supporting cast. No matter how hard he worked, the results didn't come. He sank into a deep depression for the first time in his life. He needed the job, but he desperately wanted to walk away. He didn't care if he ever worked again. He didn't care about anything. He begged God for release. But God said, "No. You work for Me. I am your provider. Stay where you are and give *Me* your best."

He wrestled with God. *No, God. I'm really done. Can't You see? I don't care anymore. I can't do this.* Morning after morning, he woke up to the same darkness. *Release me, God!* But instead of providing an escape, God gave him the grace to keep working. He led him to an encouraging doctor who understood situational depression. "This will pass," she said confidently. She prescribed medication that took the edge off the darkness. While it made no sense to keep working in a toxic environment where he was set up for failure, he devoted himself to giving the Lord his very best in the midst of it. The results still didn't come, but God had something better. Through the care and ministry of close, believing friends, God revealed that Jeff had allowed a lifetime of work achievements to define his identity and self-worth. Then He spoke a profound life-changing truth that hit home: "You are My beloved son, regardless of your earthly failures and successes." Finally, God released him. The employer let him go.

Over the next six months of healing and restoration, God's voice became clear again. Yes, He was still calling him to the marketplace. He wasn't finished with him yet! Only this time, his identity and position were secure in Christ alone. He knew he was a son of God, and no amount of success or failure would alter that fact. He interviewed for many promising opportunities, and each time he learned he was not selected and all the voices said, "You're too old," a peace surrounded him like he had never known before, a confidence that God's plans and timing are perfect. "God will provide the right job," Jeff assured his wife. And God did. Shortly after his sixty-third birthday, he became a market sales leader for an established company who needed and valued his experience and wisdom. As he drives each morning the few short miles to corporate headquarters, he is filled with wonder at the faithfulness of the God who rewarded his obedience. He would indeed finish well. Because God not only provided; He saved His best for last.

Seek First His Kingdom

Seek the Kingdom of God above all else, and live righteously,
and he will give you everything you need.
MATTHEW 6:33

Matthew sat with the others on the mountainside near Capernaum, his hometown. The Teacher had called His first followers together to give them clear instructions for living in this Kingdom He spoke about. He had covered many topics over the past few days. He taught them about the traits He was looking for in His followers and how He was preparing them to make a positive difference in the world. He taught about obedience to the law and how He had come to fulfill it through love and reverence for God. He taught them about anger, lust, and divorce, and about loving their enemies instead of seeking revenge. He taught them to give to the needy and to pray and fast. And He taught them about money.

Now money was something Matthew knew about. He was a despised tax collector when Jesus chose him. Tax collectors were notoriously corrupt, known for collecting more than was owed to the Roman government—after all, he had to make a living. His fellow Jews considered him a traitor, and it was scandalous and offensive for Jesus to have chosen him. But Jesus saw something more. Instead of collecting taxes, Matthew would be collecting souls.

Matthew leaned in as Jesus taught His followers to "store their treasures in heaven where moths and rust cannot destroy, and thieves do not break in and steal" and warned that they "cannot serve God and be enslaved to money." What a contrast to sitting in his tax booth on the main highway scheming to line his pockets by overcharging farmers and merchants the tax they owed on imported goods. Yes, he had allowed wealth and possessions to dominate his thought life and to be his master—and the more he collected, the more he wanted.

But now, things were different. Now, he served a different Master. This Master told him not to worry about everyday life—whether he had enough food and drink, or enough clothes to wear. He pointed at the birds, who don't plant or harvest or store food in barns, and yet His heavenly Father feeds them. "Aren't you far more valuable to Him than they are?" He asked. He pointed at the lilies of the field and how they grow, how they don't work or make their clothing, and marveled that Solomon in all his glory was not dressed as beautifully as they were. "If God cares so wonderfully for wildflowers that are here today and thrown into the fire tomorrow, He will certainly care for you," He said confidently.

"Why do you have so little faith? Can all your worries add a single moment to your life?" He challenged. "These things dominate the thoughts of unbelievers, but your heavenly Father already knows all your needs. Seek the Kingdom of God above all else, and live righteously, and He will give you everything you need. Don't worry about tomorrow, for tomorrow will bring its own worries. Today's trouble is enough for today."

Matthew marveled at the Teacher's words. On the surface, it seemed like he was trading a life of wealth and security for a life of poverty and uncertainty. But somehow he knew he had been called into something more. Something eternal—a life of complete trust in the One who would supply his every need—the Creator and Sustainer of life itself. (Based on Matthew 6:19–34.)

Jesus provided practical teaching in the Sermon on the Mount to Matthew and other followers who had committed their lives to Him, just as He is speaking to us today. There is a good reason He addressed worry in His teaching about money. Surveys show that Americans think more about money on a daily basis than about anything else.[1] We worry about keeping and finding a job, paying for groceries, paying the rent or making the house payment, paying for healthcare, saving for retirement, and the list goes on. He knows how we worry about money. But He makes it abundantly clear we are not to be anxious over the basic needs He promises to supply.

He made it clear that the same God who breathed life into you would sustain it. He can be trusted to handle basic details like food, clothing, and shelter (Matthew 6:25). You don't have to fret and fear tomorrow, because He cares deeply about you and holds the future in His hands (Matthew 6:26, 28–30, 34). Worrying about money and possessions can take a toll on your health, reveals a lack of trust in God's nature, and can cause you to doubt His Word. He already knows what you need, but worry holds you captive to the lie that you can't trust Him to provide (Matthew 6:31–33). It causes you to live by the limitations and rules of the world instead of the power and promises of the Kingdom.

Jesus is not denying your situation is challenging. He is not teaching laziness or poor planning. He is not telling you to sit on the couch and wait for your ship to come in. He makes it very clear that we are to work for a living (2 Thessalonians 3:11–12).

1. "2015 Life + Money Survey," *GO BankingRates*, September 9, 2015, http://cdn. gobankingrates.com/wp-content/uploads/2015/09/What-Americans-Think-Most-About-2015-Life-Money-Survey-GOBankingRates.pdf.

But He doesn't want you to strive and worry to make ends meet or fight to accumulate wealth and possessions on your own power. He wants you to trust Him. He is inviting you into an intimate relationship that comes only from spending time with Him and fully depending on Him for your every need. He wants you to hold loosely to the things that fade, wear out, or get used up, and to focus on the things that last forever. Because God has made you a promise; if you seek His Kingdom above all else, the rest will fall into place. He *will* give you everything you need.

Prayer

Lord, forgive me for obsessing over money and possessions instead of You. I don't want to be held captive by the material things of this world that are here today and gone tomorrow. I want to be held captive only by You and Your love for me. You are the only master I want to serve. Show me how to hold loosely onto the things of this world! Help me to keep my eyes focused on You alone.

Lord, forgive me for worrying and fretting about the things You promise to provide. You are the Creator of the universe and I can trust You with the details of my life. You care for the birds, who don't plant or harvest or store food in barns. You dress the lilies of the field in splendor, and they don't work or make their clothing. How much more will You care for me? You won't ignore those who depend on You. Help me to believe it, Lord! You already know all my needs, and You hold my future in Your hands. I give You all my tomorrows, Lord. Help me to trust You. Help me to seek You first.

Our Daily Bread

"Give us each day our daily bread."
LUKE 11:3 NIV

There was once a man named Adam who lived in a redeemed land where a kind and loving king cared for his subjects. On the land were large storehouses containing everything they needed to live comfortably. Each day they were to make their requests to the king, and he would send messengers out to deliver their supplies. There was only one other condition—when the king's messenger arrived, they must be found waiting and ready to receive the delivery. But Adam lived in poverty while all his neighbors lived in plenty. One day, a messenger took him to the storehouse and showed him all the packages of daily provision and gifts of favor addressed to his home. Sadly, he never received them because he never stood watch and answered the door. Adam finally came to enjoy all the blessings of living in the land by learning how to petition and wait on the king for his daily needs.[2]

Just as this kind and loving king cared for his subjects, our heavenly Father cares for us. In the Sermon on the Mount, when He taught us to pray, "give us this day our daily bread," He wanted us to know that He alone is the provider and the sustainer of life. As Creator, He knows what we need, and we can trust Him to give us our day's share (Matthew 6:34). Like a child depends on a parent to meet his daily needs, we can depend on our heavenly Father. Asking for our daily provision ensures

2. Emily Steele Elliot, *Expectation Corner* (Palm Springs, CA: Merchant Books, 2013).

our dependence on Him and keeps us in a place of intimacy and communication.

Sometimes, we can be like Adam. We may find ourselves living in poverty in a land of plenty. Maybe we don't request what we need because we feel unworthy. We think God won't provide for our needs because of our shortcomings and past mistakes. Sometimes we lift up halfhearted prayers because we don't want to be disappointed if God doesn't answer. We don't want to get our hopes up, so in a sense, we give God an out. We pray without expecting to receive. When God comes with the answer, He finds the house dark and the door closed. Like Adam, we can't receive what we don't expect to receive. Sometimes, we just get tired of waiting or decide we can do better on our own. We stop asking altogether or we rush out ahead of God and take matters into our own hands. We work and strive to store up our own supply, drift away from the Source of our blessing, or get lost altogether. Instead of waiting for Him to deliver His best, we settle for much less and wonder why things aren't working out the way we had hoped.

Beloved, if this is you, know that you are a redeemed child of God and there is no condemnation in Him (Romans 8:1)! He has set you apart and is waiting to lavish His unlimited love and provision on you. As a citizen of His Kingdom, you are entitled to all His blessings. You can rest assured that when you make a request for your daily needs, the King hears and the King will answer. Sometimes the answer might be different than you expect or it might take longer than you would like for your supply to come, but it *will* come and it will always be the King's very best. Day by day, bring Him your requests and wait expectantly (Psalm 5:3). Don't worry about anything, and thank Him for all He has done (Philippians 4:6). Then stand watch at the door and be ready to receive. There is no shortage in His heavenly treasury (Deuteronomy 28:12). He will meet all your needs according to the richness of His glory (Philippians 4:19). His storehouse is full of packages and promises addressed just to you.

Prayer

Listen to my voice in the morning, Lord. Each morning I bring my requests to You and wait expectantly (Psalm 5:3)! Thank You for hearing my prayers and promising to provide everything I need. Help me to wait expectantly to receive all the blessings You have in store for me. You are my Provider, the sustainer of life! Help me to depend on You for my daily supply, as a child depends on an earthly parent.

Thank You, Lord, for making me worthy to receive! Forgive me when I've failed to trust You, stepped out ahead of You, or taken matters into my own hands. Help me to wait for my supply to come even when I see no messenger on the horizon! Lord, I know You want the best for me. There is no lack in Your heavenly storehouse. You have a day's share promised just for me. Help me to trust You, Lord. I give You all my doubt and my worry. Give me this day my daily bread!

A Good, Good Father

"So if you sinful people know how to give good gifts to
your children, how much more will your heavenly Father
give the Holy Spirit to those who ask him."
LUKE 11:13

His disciples sat on the mountainside with the rest of the crowd, listening attentively to the Teacher. He had been speaking for hours, or maybe it was days. No one seemed to care. His teaching was unlike any they had heard before, almost a direct contradiction to their typical way of life. At one point, one of His disciples stood and said, "Lord, teach us to pray." So He gave them a model prayer, a pattern for praising God, praying for His work in the world, and for helping them through the daily struggles they all would face as His followers. In this prayer, He taught them to honor and respect God's majestic and holy name. He taught them that His Kingdom had come and His perfect purpose could be accomplished on earth as it was in heaven. He taught them to trust God daily to meet their needs, to help them recognize temptation, and to give them strength to overcome it. He taught them that forgiveness was the cornerstone of prayer, and they must grant the same forgiveness to others as He had granted them (Matthew 6:9–15; Luke 11:2–4).

And then He paused. The disciples sensed He would tell a story as He so often did to illustrate His teaching. "Suppose you went to a friend's house at midnight, wanting to borrow three loaves of bread," He said. "You say to him, 'A friend of mine has just arrived for a visit, and I have nothing for him to eat.' And suppose he calls out from his bedroom, 'Don't bother me. The door is locked for the night, and my family and I are all in bed.

I can't help you.' But I tell you this—though he won't do it for friendship's sake, if you keep knocking long enough, he will get up and give you whatever you need because of your shameless persistence."

He paused again, waiting for them to digest His words. And then He explained the point of the illustration: "And so I tell you, keep on asking, and you will receive what you ask for. Keep on seeking, and you will find. Keep on knocking, and the door will be opened to you. For everyone who asks, receives. Everyone who seeks, finds. And to everyone who knocks, the door will be opened."

To further emphasize His point, He added, "You fathers—if your children ask for a fish, do you give them a snake instead? Or if they ask for an egg, do you give them a scorpion? Of course not! So if you sinful people know how to give good gifts to your children, how much more will your heavenly Father give the Holy Spirit to those who ask Him." (Based on Luke 11:5–13.)

In this story about the man who wouldn't get out of bed to help a friend, Jesus is teaching us the importance of persistent prayer. Continuing to ask, seek, and knock until God answers your prayer is more for your benefit than His. He knows already your needs, and His timing is perfect. Our persistent prayer helps us better understand the intensity of our need and dependence on God and deepens our pursuit of Him. Unfortunately, when we don't receive according to our timetable or in the way we expect, we often give up after a few halfhearted attempts. We conclude He is not a good Father who can be trusted to meet our needs, but a distant Father who doesn't care and has left us to fend for ourselves.

If you are a parent, would you leave your children to fend for themselves? Would you give them snakes and scorpions when they asked for fish and eggs? Of course not. Jesus wants us to understand that if fallible human parents can be so kind and loving, how much more so is our Father in heaven, the Creator and giver of all things good (1 Timothy 1:4; James 1:17)! Father God is not selfish and stingy, and you don't have to beg Him to meet your needs (Psalm 84:11). He protects you when you think you're asking for fish, and you're really asking for snakes! He is a good Father who understands your needs and wants the very best for you.

Getting to a place of full dependence requires you to relentlessly pursue God. Keep on asking, keep on seeking, and keep on knocking. As you grow in your knowledge of Him and His nature, your requests will be more aligned with His heart. Jesus assures us He will reward such shameless persistence. The door is sure to be opened to you, and you will receive what you ask for. Because He is a good, good Father.

Prayer

Lord, thank You for teaching me how to pray, for giving me a pattern to follow to pray for Your work in the world and to pray through the daily struggles I face as a Christ-follower. I praise You, Lord. I want to know You. I want to know Your heart. Help me to persist shamelessly in prayer like this man seeking to borrow bread. Give me what I need to keep on asking, keep on seeking, and keep on knocking!

Forgive me when I've given up because I haven't received from You on my timetable and I've misunderstood Your nature and love for me. I know You have a plan for my life, and You always want the very best for me. Thank You for protecting me when I unknowingly ask for snakes and scorpions! Yes, Lord. I want to know You. I want to chase after You in relentless pursuit until my heart and Yours beat as one, until I fully trust You to meet my every need. You are a good, good Father. Open the door, Lord. I receive.

Window Shopping

For as he thinks in his heart, so is he.
PROVERBS 23:7 AMP

No matter what he did, John couldn't get ahead. He could pay the bills (barely), but he always worried about what he would do if something really big happened. . .like his twenty-five-year-old furnace going out. Or the roof needing replacing. Not to mention sending his three kids to college and trying to save whatever scraps were left for retirement. Things were not likely to change. He was passed over for the last three promotions at work. No matter. He hated his job anyway, and his boss was a jerk. His wife thought it might be time to look for another job. But why bother? Who can find a decent job in this economy?

Cindy loved clothes. And shoes. And hats, purses, jewelry, accessories, and. . .well, she had lots. *Lots.* Her friends called her the ultimate "fashionista" and looked to her for the latest fashion trends. Occasionally her husband would complain: "Do you *really* need more clothes? Don't you have enough?" And she would always remind him that his toys and hobbies cost a lot more than her little clothes habit. Besides, they could afford it. And she had a reputation to uphold.

Both John and Cindy hold an underlying belief of lack and insufficiency, and their thoughts have influenced who they have become. This mindset of poverty is not limited to money and material things. A rich person can be held captive by a poverty mindset, while someone can be dirt poor and live a grateful, generous life and feel they lack nothing. A poverty mindset is an attitude rooted in our identity, where we believe certain lies about God and ourselves. We may have underlying beliefs such as, "There is never enough for me because I'm not worth it," "God doesn't care about me," or "God can't be trusted to provide for my needs." These attitudes are often fueled by fears such as failure, insufficiency, rejection, or abandonment. For example, earthly fathers provide for their children and give them security and value. If a father leaves the family or a child's basic needs are unmet, they may believe the lie that Father God won't meet their needs either and it's all up to them to take care of themselves. Continual rejection may lead to apathy and a false belief that I am not worthy to receive. Or it may lead to the opposite: If I just work harder, acquire more, or be more successful or perfect, then I'll be worthy.

People with this mindset may have grown up in a home where money was considered the "root of all evil," wealthy people were resented, or caregivers repeatedly told them they were poor or couldn't afford things, whether or not their needs were being met. All of these experiences and false beliefs impact our feelings of self-worth, our ability to trust God to meet our needs, and knowing our identity as a child of God who is loved and valued.

A poverty mindset may express itself in many ways. Like John, we might blame others for our circumstances, whether the job, our boss, our parents, our spouse, the market, or the economy. We can live in fear from paycheck to paycheck, waiting for the worst to happen. Or we can justify our predicament by not caring about money at all. Instead of embracing hope, faith, hard work, sowing, reaping, discipline, and other biblical principles, we believe the situation we find ourselves in is not our fault and we are powerless to change it. We complain about everything and become a perpetual victim of our circumstances. Or like Cindy, we collect things to prove our value and worth, not realizing that God is the true source of our material need and the only One who can satisfy the deep void in our soul, the One who died to make us worthy.

The good news is that God can renew your mind and change the way you think (Romans 12:2)! He can replace the lies you have believed with the truth. A renewed mindset can make all the difference in how you respond to your circumstances. Start by surrendering your thought life to Jesus. Take every thought captive to His authority (2 Corinthians 10:4–6). Instead of living in fear, you can be anxious for nothing (Philippians 4:6). Instead of feeling powerless, your strength is in Christ (Philippians 4:13). Instead of believing He is a distant Father who orphaned you, you know He is a loving God who cares for you (1 Peter 5:6–7). You no longer go through life like John, a window-shopper who only dreams about owning the expensive items behind the glass. Or like Cindy, buying everything you see to fill the God-sized hole in your heart. Your mindset has changed, and you know who you are. You are a child of the King, and you lack nothing.

Prayer

Lord, sometimes I can relate to John and Cindy. I have focused on what I lack instead of what I have! I have blamed others for my circumstances, lived in fear over my finances, felt powerless to change, and doubted Your promise to provide. And yes, I have complained! Forgive me, Lord!

Lord, forgive me for believing the lies that there is never enough, that I am not worth it, and that You won't care for me. I receive the truth that You are a God of abundance, a loving Father who cares for me. I can trust You to meet my every need. Thank You for renewing my mind and changing the way I think! Thank You for all You have done for me. Only You can fill the God-hole in my heart. Only You can satisfy. You are enough.

Throw Out Your Net

*Then he said, "Throw out your net on the right-hand side of the boat,
and you'll get some!" So they did, and they couldn't haul
in the net because there were so many fish in it.*

JOHN 21:6

Peter, Thomas, Nathanael, James, John, and two other disciples sat in stunned silence trying to make sense of the events of the past few weeks. First, the nightmare of Jesus' arrest and horrific death, followed by the indescribable wonder of His resurrection; it was more than they could possibly take in. *What now? What's next for us?*

Restless and not knowing what else to do, Peter suddenly jumped up and said, "I'm going fishing." It sounded like a good idea. It was familiar and productive. Something they could *do.* "We'll come, too," they all said. So they all climbed in the boat and went out to fish. All night long, they threw out the net and pulled it back in. Cast and pull, cast and pull, cast and pull. Nothing. Each time the net came back empty, they grew more discouraged. After all, they were fishermen! It was their work, their livelihood, and they hadn't caught a single fish! *What kind of fishermen are we? What now? What's next for us?*

At dawn they could see someone standing on the beach. A friendly voice called out, "Fellows, have you caught any fish?" "No," they replied. Then he said, "Throw out your net on the right-hand side of the boat, and you'll get some!" Without a word, they cast their net on the other side. This time when they pulled on the net, they couldn't haul it in because there were so many fish in it!

The scene was strangely familiar. Once before someone had

instructed them where to fish. That time, they caught so many fish their nets began to tear and their boats almost sank! And then John knew. "It's the Lord!" he shouted to Peter. Without a second thought, Peter put on his tunic, jumped into the water, and swam toward the Lord. The others stayed with the boat and began pulling the loaded net toward the shore. They were only about a hundred yards away. As they drew closer, the sight and smells captured their senses, reminding them how tired, cold, and hungry they were. Breakfast was waiting—delicious fish cooking over a charcoal fire and some bread.

Peter had arrived ahead of them. Greeting him, Jesus said, "Bring some of the fish you've just caught." So Peter went to the boat and dragged the net to the shore. It was heavy. In it were 153 large fish, to be exact. And unlike before, the net hadn't torn. Jesus threw more fish on the fire and said, "Now come and have some breakfast!" So they all sat down by the warm fire, and Jesus served them the bread and the fish. This was the third time He had appeared to them since He had been raised from the dead. As they ate, they pondered. *What now? What's next for us?* Soon they would know. (Based on John 21:14; Luke 5:4–7.)

––––––––––––––––––

Sometimes your best efforts don't seem to make a difference. You are working hard, fishing off the right side of the boat, but you never seem to catch a break. It never seems to be enough. No matter what you do, you can't climb out of debt, achieve your goals, or move into your destiny. Like Jesus' first disciples, maybe you're bewildered by your circumstances and waiting for clarity and direction. Or you're waiting for your circumstances to change or to be released altogether. You know He wants the best for you, but you don't understand His timing or His purposes.

You don't understand what He's doing right now. Jesus wants you to trust Him, regardless of your circumstances. So you keep fishing. You keep doing what you've always done. And your net keeps coming up empty.

And then suddenly, He comes. He tells you what to do. He tells you to throw your net on the other side. Do things differently. Trust Him, even though it seems counterintuitive, and see what He can do. You may hear His audible voice or conviction in your spirit. He may speak through a friend, pastor, or someone you trust. However He speaks to you, you just *know* He's releasing you to make a course correction. And He may be telling you to do it now. Peter and the disciples were fishermen by trade. All night long they cast their nets, yet they caught nothing. But once again they discovered that Jesus was in complete control of their destiny, working on their behalf, even when they didn't understand. He had the ultimate power over their work, the boat, the net, the sea, the fish, and time itself. And they learned once again that obedience to His guidance and direction can transform failure into success.

There are seasons of confusion when your net keeps coming up empty and all you can do is keep on fishing and keep on waiting. You may grow weary, cold, wet, hungry, and discouraged. And then morning comes, and He is there standing on the shore, guiding your next move, inviting you to sit by the warm fire, and feeding you breakfast. Beloved, when it's time to make a course correction, trust He will let you know. Then throw out your net and haul in your big catch.

Prayer

Lord, I work so hard, but my nets keep coming up empty. No matter what I do, I can't seem to move forward. I don't understand what You're doing right now. But I trust You, Lord. Help me to keep on fishing and to wait patiently for Your guidance. Thank You, Lord, that when I feel lost, I can know I have not lost You!

Lord, I know You have the power and wisdom to transform my failure into success. You alone control my destiny. When it's time to make a course correction, I trust You will let me know. I may be tired and hungry, but You are a compassionate Shepherd who cares for His sheep. You care for me, Lord. Every day I feast on the abundance of Your house; I drink from Your river of delights (Psalm 36:8). Every day You feed me breakfast!

Jehovah-Jireh: Margaret's Story

The pastor came in the room and greeted her warmly. Margaret sat with her arms crossed, her eyes glaring at the latest in a long line of counselors, pastors, and religious people who would try convincing God to unlock the door to everything He had withheld from her. That is, if He was there at all. None of these people had answers. They counseled and prayed to no avail. *A waste of time*, she thought ruefully. But here she was again. "Hello," she replied icily.

She had already met the other woman in the room, a prayer minister who would be taking notes and "interceding" throughout the session. Whatever that meant. A friend had recommended that she schedule this meeting; a *Sozo* session they called it. It was something about freedom and getting rid of the negative thoughts that held her back. Well, she certainly had plenty of those, and she was certainly being held back. Her feet might as well be set in concrete.

The pastor had settled into the chair across from her. She explained a few things about the session and what to expect and asked her a few questions. Then, almost as if she already knew the answer, she leaned forward, fixed her eyes on Margaret, and gently asked, "What is one thing you want to get from our time today?" Without a thought, the words came out: "I don't want to be angry anymore." There. She said it. The rage she felt was paralyzing. Years and years of anger had reached a boiling point. No, she was years past the boiling point.

More small talk. And then the pastor asked, "Margaret, what is your view of Father God?" Surprised, she responded, "What do you mean?" The pastor clarified, "Where is He? What does He look like to you? Can you sense Him for me?" Margaret responded flatly, "I don't know what He looks like. I suppose He's sitting on a big throne somewhere busy doing important things." The pastor jotted some notes down and asked again, "Margaret, what do you think God thinks of you?" "Well, obviously not much. Sometimes I wonder if He remembers I'm alive," Margaret said coolly.

The pastor continued to probe: "Tell me about your dad. Is he still alive?" Margaret shrugged and responded, "Yes, but I don't see him much." The questions continued, and Margaret shared more. Dad hurt his back when she was young, so he didn't work much. He watched a lot of TV and drank beer. He wasn't mean. He just never had much to say. Mom was the breadwinner. She worked as a waitress to make ends meet, often double shifts. When Margaret complained she was never home, her mom would always say, "Well, someone has to work around here." She drummed it into Margaret's head that she must work hard, get good grades, go to college, and get a high-paying job. Otherwise she would end up like her mom, living from paycheck to paycheck, trapped in this dumpy little house.

Margaret never thought the house was dumpy. It was modest. And she always had enough food on the table and clothes to wear. Of course, it was nothing like her best friend, Cindy. Cindy had everything: a big house, the beautiful bedroom Margaret always wanted, and lots and lots of clothes. And really nice parents. She liked spending time at Cindy's. So she had made a vow to herself. She would never end up like her mom, scratching and clawing to make ends meet. She worked hard to get through college and earned a degree in business. She had big plans to climb the corporate ladder of success.

Then the pastor said, "Margaret, I want you to ask God, 'Lord, am I angry? Who am I angry at?'" Before Margaret could repeat the words, the floodgates burst open: "Cindy! It's always Cindy!" The words tumbled out. Now it seems, Cindy has her own big house—and a perfect husband, two perfect kids, and a perfect dog. Everything always goes perfectly for Cindy. "And I still have nothing," Margaret wept bitterly. "I keep working hard and nothing ever changes. I have the same dead-end job I landed out of college. No husband. Nothing. And where is God in all this? It's not fair!"

The pastor moved closer. "I'm so sorry, Margaret," she said softly. Then she explained how our family relationships and the lies we learn growing up can influence our view of God and His goodness. She explained how forgiveness could set her free and draw her closer to God. Guided through a series of prayers, Margaret forgave her dad for not being emotionally available throughout her childhood, for not being able to provide for her and make her feel secure. She gave up the lie that Father God would treat her the same way, that He is cold, distant, disengaged, and unable to care for her. Instead, God showed her the truth—that she is His precious child, worthy of His love and protection, and could trust Him to provide all her needs.

She forgave her mom for never being home, for being too busy, and for not being the mom she needed her to be. She gave up the lie that the Holy Spirit was anything like her mom, that she could never find rest in Him, and that He had deserted her, leaving her to trust only herself and her own hard work to make ends meet. She received the truth that the Holy Spirit was never too busy to provide for her, nurture her, and comfort her. She didn't have to work harder to receive His love and acceptance.

Through the prayer session, the Holy Spirit helped her see that fear was at the root of her anger and feelings of rejection. She asked forgiveness for allowing fear of lack and insufficiency to torment her and for agreeing with the lie that God had rejected her and forgotten about her. She repented of not trusting God to meet her needs and cast out spirits of fear, rejection, and poverty. She broke off generational mindsets that provision was up to her alone. In return, God showed her that He was her provider and she was worthy to receive.

Finally, she forgave Cindy for always having more. She asked God's forgiveness for jealousy and for harboring bitterness and offense against her friend. She released Cindy into His hands; it was not up to her to judge how God blesses another person or to compare herself with someone else.

Then, at the pastor's prompting, she reached out her hands and gave God her anger. In her mind's eye, she saw herself setting down all the ugliness at His feet. In an instant, it started burning. And then it was gone. At that very moment, an amazing feeling of peace rushed in, and love wrapped its arms around her like a secure blanket. The burden had lifted. Years and years of anger were gone. She left the church that day feeling lighter. . .whole. . .free. Her situation hadn't changed, but her mindset was different. Instead of feeling rejected and overlooked, she had complete security in her identity as a child of God. Instead of lack and insufficiency, she felt overwhelming contentment and a new trust in Jehovah-Jireh, the God who provides.

Two Pennies

"I tell you the truth, this poor widow has given more than all the others who are making contributions. For they gave a tiny part of their surplus, but she, poor as she is, has given everything she had to live on."
MARK 12:43–44

While teaching and preaching the Good News in the Temple one day, the religious leaders and teachers of the law challenged Jesus by asking several trick questions. He answered each one with such authority that no one dared ask any more. Then, with the crowds listening, He turned to His disciples and said, "Beware of these teachers of religious law! For they like to parade around in flowing robes and receive respectful greetings as they walk in the marketplaces. And how they love the seats of honor in the synagogues and the head table at banquets. Yet they shamelessly cheat widows out of their property and then pretend to be pious by making long prayers in public. Because of this, they will be more severely punished."

Pondering these words, the disciples walked with Him to the area across from the Temple treasury and stopped for a moment to take in the scene. They were in the Court of Women where worshippers and religious people gathered to make their donations. Seven collection boxes were designated for worshippers to pay the Temple Tax, and six boxes were allotted for free-will offerings. Jesus sat down near one of the collection boxes and watched as the crowds dropped in their money.

A small figure appeared. She contrasted starkly with the wealthy people in their fine dress, who dropped large amounts of money in the collection boxes as they lingered in conversation with each other. She pulled at her head covering to secure it closer to her face as she scurried through the crowd. It made no sense for her to come. She didn't belong here with all these rich people. She was a poor defenseless widow with nothing to give. They would probably mock her. Yet something compelled her. Stopping at one of the boxes for the free-will offerings, she began digging in her skirts. Finding what she was looking for, she dropped two small coins into the collection box. She paused for a moment, turned on her heels, and began weaving her way out through the crowd the same way she'd come.

Watching her in amazement, Jesus called His disciples to Him and said, "I tell you the truth, this poor widow has given more than all the others who are making contributions. For they gave a tiny part of their surplus, but she, poor as she is, has given everything she had to live on." (Based on Mark 12:38–44.)

The Bible instructs us to give back to God what He has graciously given us in the form of a tithe (Genesis 14:19–20; 28:20–22; Proverbs 3:9–10; Malachi 3:10–12). Matthew records that Jesus rebuked the Pharisees for taking care to tithe even the tiniest income from their herb gardens, while they ignored the more important aspects of the law—justice, mercy, and faith (Matthew 23:23). Here again in this story, Jesus exposed their evil hearts. Behind the appearance of holiness and respectability, they were selfish, religious hypocrites. According to Jewish law, they received no pay; they depended on the offerings of devout Jews. But many took advantage of this custom, using it to cheat the poor and take advantage of the rich. Through their pious actions, they hoped to gain honor, status, and recognition. But their religious actions did not cancel out sin. Jesus warned that their punishment would be severe because they abused their authority. Instead of guiding the people's faith and demonstrating mercy and justice, they saddled them with petty rules and exploited their devotion to God.

At the Temple that day, Jesus watched as the rich dropped large sums of money into the collection boxes. But from God's perspective, the widow's meager gift of two pennies to the Temple was not only the smallest, but more than all the gifts from the rich put together. Widows were counted among the poorest, voiceless, and most vulnerable in Jewish society. She was not only poor, but she had few resources for making money. Her gift was a huge sacrifice, likely all she had, but she gave it willingly. Jesus not only praised her, but noted the injustice of her circumstances. The gap between the rich and poor still exists in our society today. Yet, how often do we consider ourselves generous when we give a small percentage of our total income or a "tiny part of our surplus?" How often do those with the least give the most?

The heart motives behind our offerings are much more important than the amount. We should never give simply to follow the law, to gain status and recognition, to be seen as or feel more "spiritual," or to get something in return. Jesus made this clear when He praised the poor widow's giving after rebuking the religious leaders for shamelessly cheating people like her out of their property, all while pretending to be pious. Our gifts are pleasing to God when given out of a heart bursting with gratitude and love for the Father for all He has done (Colossians 2:7). There was no other way for this widow to give. The religious leaders should have been taking care of people like her. But she put her trust in a higher power. She gave her two pennies to the God who provides.

Prayer

Lord, forgive me when I've given from a wrong heart—to meet expectations, gain recognition or status, or expecting something in return. Forgive me when I've given out of guilt and condemnation! Lord, this woman did not give reluctantly or out of pressure, but cheerfully (2 Corinthians 9:7). She gave all that she had to One who had given His all to her. Lord, help my giving overflow from a place of true generosity, a heart that is devoted to You, and for no other reason.

Lord, You alone are my Provider. I trust You will supply all I need from Your glorious riches. All I have is Yours. Help me see any injustice around me through Your eyes. Break my heart for the things that break Yours. You have shown me mercy, Lord. Help me show Your mercy to others.

Full Barns

"Yes, a person is a fool to store up earthly wealth
but not have a rich relationship with God."
LUKE 12:21

A huge crowd had gathered to hear Him preach in Judea. Thousands pressed in, trampling one another, as Jesus spoke against the hypocrisy of the Pharisees and warned of blasphemy against the Holy Spirit. His message was challenging and not all in the crowd were friendly. He was teaching them not to worry about the persecution they would face as His followers when someone interrupted Him, calling out from the crowd, "Teacher, please tell my brother to divide our father's estate with me!"

Now it was not unusual for disputes like this to be brought to the rabbis to settle, although the man's timing was more than inappropriate. Unfazed by the rude interruption and sudden change of topic, Jesus replied, "Friend, who made Me a judge over you to decide such things as that?" Then, not waiting for an answer, he said, "Beware! Guard against every kind of greed. Life is not measured by how much you own." He watched as the crowd pondered this bold statement that was so contrary to their culture and way of life.

Then He told them a story: "A rich man had a fertile farm that produced fine crops. He said to himself, 'What should I do? I don't have room for all my crops.' Then he said, 'I know! I'll tear down my barns and build bigger ones. Then I'll have room enough to store all my wheat and other goods. And I'll sit back and say to myself, "My friend, you have enough stored away for years to come. Now take it easy! Eat, drink, and be merry!" But God said to him, 'You fool! You will die this very night. Then who will get everything you worked for?'" Pausing to see the crowd's reaction, Jesus summarized His point: "Yes, a person is a fool to store up earthly wealth but not have a rich relationship with God." (Based on Luke 12:13–21.)

Sometimes, like with this man, we cry out to God to fix a problem, and He wants us to work on our attitude toward the problem instead. In this case, Jesus didn't help the man resolve his inheritance problem. Instead, He responded by pointing to a higher issue—the man's attitude toward the wealth he stood to inherit. But Jesus used this opportunity to teach the crowd that having a good life has nothing to do with being wealthy and accumulating possessions. Our relationship with God is far more important. He illustrated His point by telling them a story.

The first thing we notice about this rich man is how his focus was always on himself. There were a lot of *I*'s and *my*'s in his planning process and nothing about God: "What should *I* do, *my* crops, *my* barns, *my* wheat." He seems to have forgotten the One who truly owned his corps, barns, and goods (Psalm 24:1). Thinking ahead wasn't the problem. Saving for the future and planning for retirement is wise. But he failed to plan for his eternal future. He focused on accumulating wealth he could never take with him with no regard for others. He came into this world empty-handed, and he was about to leave empty-handed (1 Timothy 6:7). He thought he was rich, but in the end he was broke. Jesus challenges us to think beyond our worldly goals. We may spend time, energy, and focus on accumulating wealth, but we should always have the same rich desire for God. When we truly understand the Source of our blessing, our love and gratefulness compel us to share with others to advance His Kingdom. We don't build bigger barns.

We store our treasures in heaven (Matthew 6:20).

It's true, we live in a world that values nice things. Advertisers spend millions to convince us we don't have enough, and accumulating more will bring happiness, fulfillment, and comfort. The problem isn't having things. It's all about whether or not we have God. We can spend a lifetime filling our barns with wealth and possessions, and building bigger barns, only to discover we still feel empty and unsatisfied. That's because He gave each of us a great big God-sized hole inside that only He can fill. It was part of His plan for you to live in a rich relationship with Him, so He hardwired it right into your DNA. When you have Him, you can rest assured; your barns are always full.

Prayer

Lord, I can come to You with a list of wants, and You always have a way of putting Your finger on what I truly need. My relationship with You is more important than anything I think I need today. You alone are all I need, Lord. Only You can fill the empty places in my heart. Help me store my riches in heaven. Help me store my riches in You.

Thank You, Lord, for all the blessings You have poured on me! Forgive me for the times I've lost my way and chased after wealth and possessions instead of You. Help me hold on loosely to my earthly plans to accumulate financial security. I know my eternal security is in You alone! Bring me back in alignment, Lord! Only You can truly satisfy. When I have You, I have everything. When I have You, my barns are always full.

Well Done

"To those who use well what they are given, even more will be given,
and they will have an abundance. But from those who do nothing,
even what little they have will be taken away."
MATTHEW 25:29

The disciples were deeply concerned. As usual, they didn't understand. They had hoped for a political leader who would establish an earthly kingdom and free them from the oppressive Roman government. Now, Jesus tells them the Temple would be demolished? When would this happen? Would there be the sign of His return and the end of the world? As they sat on the slopes of the Mount of Olives, He prepared them for what was to come. He would depart, but He would return again. He assured them the date was not important. Instead, they must focus on being prepared, remaining watchful, and doing His work here on earth—building and expanding God's Kingdom.

And then, as He so often did, He told them a story to illustrate: A man was going on a long trip so he called his servants together and entrusted his money to them while he was gone. "He gave five bags of silver to one, two bags of silver to another, and one bag of silver to the last—dividing it in proportion to their abilities. He then left on his trip," Jesus explained. "The servant who received the five bags of silver began to invest the money and earned five more. The servant with two bags of silver also went to work and earned two more. But the servant who received the one bag of silver dug a hole in the ground and hid the master's money."

He paused to let them consider the scenario and then continued with the rest of the story: "After a long time their master returned from his trip and called them to give an account of how they had used his money. The servant to whom he had entrusted the five bags of silver came forward with five more and said, 'Master, you gave me five bags of silver to invest, and I have earned five more.' The master was full of praise. 'Well done, my good and faithful servant. You have been faithful in handling this small amount, so now I will give you many more responsibilities. Let's celebrate together!'

"The servant who had received the two bags of silver came forward and said, 'Master, you gave me two bags of silver to invest, and I have earned two more.'

"The master said, 'Well done, my good and faithful servant. You have been faithful in handling this small amount, so now I will give you many more responsibilities. Let's celebrate together!'

"Then the servant with the one bag of silver came and said, 'Master, I knew you were a harsh man, harvesting crops you didn't plant and gathering crops you didn't cultivate. I was afraid I would lose your money, so I hid it in the earth. Look, here is your money back.' But the master replied, 'You wicked and lazy servant! If you knew I harvested crops I didn't plant and gathered crops I didn't cultivate, why didn't you deposit my money in the bank? At least I could have gotten some interest on it.' Then he ordered, 'Take the money from this servant, and give it to the one with the ten bags of silver. To those who use well what they are given, even more will be given, and they will have an abundance. But from those who do nothing, even what little they have will be taken away. Now throw this useless servant into outer darkness, where there will be weeping and gnashing of teeth.' " (Based on Matthew 25:14–30.)

In Jesus' illustration, the master's purpose was not to increase his own wealth but to see which of his servants would be worthy of greater responsibility when he returned. In the same way, Jesus, our Master, has given us gifts to invest wisely and responsibly. Our "bags of silver" are the resources He has entrusted to us, whether time, spiritual gifts, abilities, talents, and knowledge. His purpose is for us to use our gifts to glorify Him and advance His Kingdom until He returns. Just as this master gave each servant different amounts to invest, His gifts to us may not be distributed evenly, but according to our ability and purpose. He will never measure our success by how much we have, but how we used what we have been given. He cares most about our effort and our faithfulness.

Upon his return, the master didn't reward his first two servants with silver, but with greater responsibility in proportion to their faithfulness and ability to invest the amount they received. Because they were faithful in a very small thing, they showed him the ability to take on more. In contrast, the "wicked and lazy" servant played it safe and didn't even take the simplest and most conservative steps to get some increase on the money by depositing it with the banker. He deliberately did nothing that would benefit his master, and since he was given an amount he could handle, his failure only meant laziness or disdain for his master. This servant didn't share His master's goals, didn't trust His master's intentions to govern fairly, and put his own interests ahead of concern for others. As a result, the master took his silver away and gave it to the servant who invested and gained the most. The master didn't base this decision on fairness or need, but on each servant's faithfulness to use the silver he had been given.

How would you respond if the Master asked how you have used the gifts He has given you? Some of us have buried our silver because we were too busy with our own agenda. Others have grown discouraged, frustrated, or even angry at God for our regrets and failures. Some have become discouraged and afraid to risk again. Still others spend everything they have, while some live like misers. Beloved, always remember the bags of silver the Lord has given you actually belong to Him. We are merely caretakers of His resources. Wherever you might work, whether in the home, in the workplace, or as a volunteer, He is your employer and you work for Him. You can trust He will give you everything you need to do whatever work He calls you to do (Ephesians 2:10). Yes, He will hold us accountable for how we invest His silver. But when you invest it in faith out of love for the Master and devotion to His agenda, success is sure to come. When you use well what you are given, even more will you be given, and you will have an abundance. And when you meet Him face-to-face, the Master will be filled with praise: "Well done, faithful servant. Well done."

Prayer

Lord, these are hard words to hear, that those who do nothing, even what little they have will be taken away. Forgive me for making excuses for not using the gifts You have given me, for the times I've squandered, penny pinched, or simply buried my silver. I'm sorry for the times I've focused on my own purposes and ignored Yours. I'm sorry for growing discouraged, frustrated, or even angry at You for my own mistakes. Lord, You are a God of mercy and grace. Please give me courage to risk again. Please help me to trust You.

Lord, You taught the disciples to be prepared, remain watchful, and do Your work until You return. This teaching applies to me, too. Thank You for the gifts You have given me. Show me how to use my gifts for Your glory. In times of scarcity and in times of plenty, help me be a good steward of the silver You have entrusted to me. Help my agenda align with Yours. When I meet You face-to-face, I want to hear You say, "Well done."

Fat Cats

These fat cats have everything their hearts could ever wish for!
PSALM 73:7

"I'll let you know! Thank you!" Alice ended the call on her cell phone. Another family invite to her friend Jenn's cabin. They would have to miss church again, and her Saturday morning small group. She sat down at the table sipping her coffee, pondering the latest invitation.

The church had been a godsend. Her family was struggling. Sales were down at her husband's company, and they were hanging by a thread. That meant huge cuts in his commission plan and some adjustments in their spending. Tensions were high as she tried to pick up more hours at work. The kids were struggling, too. Joe, her eighth grader, was getting in trouble at school. Sadie, her sixth grader and always the easygoing one, had simply withdrawn to her room. No amount of prodding seemed to get to the root of what was going on with her.

Then Joe came home from school one Wednesday and announced he was going to church that night with his friend Patrick. They had never gotten around to finding a church. Both she and her husband had attended church when they were growing up, but they shared distant memories of hard pews, boring sermons, and clock watching. She had always felt a little guilty about not taking the kids, but their schedules were so full during the week, they really needed the time to sleep in and get things done at home.

Until Joe went to church. When Patrick's mom dropped him off that night, he was so excited. He couldn't stop talking about the "cool music," the "cool group leader," the "cool kids" who were there—the "cool" everything. Joe was going back. And the rest is history. They were now members, with both kids loving the youth program, she and her husband in small groups, both doing a little volunteering, and worshipping together every Sunday. They still struggled. Their finances were still a mess and they were working on their marriage, but something had changed. This God she remembered from her childhood as being so distant had suddenly became relevant to her everyday life. She wanted to know Him more.

Her friend Jenn had been her next-door neighbor, and they had grown close until she moved away. That was two houses and one cabin ago. They had stopped trying to keep up. Jenn and Todd had everything—new cars, new boats, a golf membership, and exotic vacations. A few times, when Alice felt courageous, she invited Jenn to church. Jenn had no interest. When Alice tried to explain what she was experiencing there, Jenn rolled her eyes and changed the subject. Often, Alice would wonder, *Why, Lord? Does all this really make a difference? Everything looks so easy for people like Jenn and Todd.* Flipping through her Bible as she sipped her coffee, her eyes were suddenly drawn to these words in Psalm 73:

> *But as for me, I almost lost my footing. My feet were slipping, and I was almost gone. For I envied the proud when I saw them prosper despite their wickedness. They seem to live such painless lives; their bodies are so healthy and strong. They don't have troubles like other people; they're not plagued with problems like everyone else. They wear pride like a jeweled necklace and clothe themselves with cruelty. These fat cats have everything their hearts could ever wish for! (Psalm 73:2–7)*

Yes, Lord! Why? And then, as if He knew exactly what she was thinking, her eyes stopped again a few verses down:

> *"What does God know?" they ask.*
> *"Does the Most High even know what's happening?"*
> *Look at these wicked people—*
> *enjoying a life of ease while their riches multiply.*
> *Did I keep my heart pure for nothing? (Psalm 73:11–13)*

And then, the answer came:

> *Then I went into your sanctuary, O God, and I finally understood the destiny of the wicked. Truly, you put them on a slippery path and send them sliding over the cliff to destruction. (Psalm 73:17–18)*

> *Yet I still belong to you; you hold my right hand. You guide me with your counsel, leading me to a glorious destiny. Whom have I in heaven but you? I desire you more than anything on earth. (Psalm 73:23–25)*

The verses penetrated her heart as if Jesus Himself sat across the kitchen table sharing her morning coffee. Regardless of her worldly circumstances, she desired Him more. Her glorious destiny was secure. She repented of her doubts and her need to know why. And then she dropped to her knees and prayed for Jenn.

Jenn wasn't cruel or wicked, but she certainly had everything her heart could wish for, a life so inviting that Alice often dreamed of trading places. God showed her that contentment and hope could be a reality now, but only when based on Him. It would not come from wealth, possessions, and a trouble-free life. The lost were sliding over a cliff to destruction, and their wealth would someday be worthless, while her reward would be wealth that lasts forever and a glorious destiny in the presence of God.

How often are we like Alice, wondering about the non-believers who have everything their hearts could wish for while we struggle to make ends meet, keep our hearts pure, and follow Jesus? Beloved, God sees what the fat cats are doing. But He cares much more about you and your relationship with Him. The apostle Paul said it best when he counted everything else as worthless garbage compared with the infinite value of knowing Jesus (Philippians 3:8). Because knowing Him is a priceless gift that can never be destroyed.

Prayer

Lord, You are so good to Your creation. You give Your sunlight to both the evil and the good, and send rain on the just and the unjust alike (Matthew 5:45). Yet, there will come a time when the evil and unjust will reap their reward, a time when the lost and their wealth will slide over the cliff to destruction. Forgive me for coveting what others have and forgetting that as a child of God, my wealth is eternal. Help me pray for the "Jenns" in my life, for the lost who put all their hopes in worldly riches instead of You.

Lord, knowing You is a priceless gift that will never compare to all the world's treasure. Thank You for guiding me with Your counsel and leading me to a glorious destiny. I desire You more than anything on earth.

Rivers of Living Water

"He who believes in Me [who adheres to, trusts in, and relies on Me],
as the Scripture has said, 'From his innermost being
will flow continually rivers of living water.'"
JOHN 7:38 AMP

John, a sales manager, had been unemployed for fourteen months. He had kids in college, his industry was downsizing, his savings were tapped out, and family health insurance benefits cost as much as his monthly mortgage. In his attempt to transition to a new industry, six consecutive job opportunities had fallen through. Being a finalist candidate was impressive, but it didn't pay the bills. Throughout his time of unemployment, he volunteered at his local church helping others like him through the job search process. God was faithful, and the job offer came just in time. Humbled and grateful, John accepted the position and continued his ministry to the unemployed.

Alan is the owner of a successful accounting practice. He started the business in his home and worked hard to establish his client base. There were many lean years where he was often tempted to get a job in an established firm. He and his family had found guidance and support through his local church, where he discovered his heart for missions. Today, he has eight accountants working for him in an office building he owns and rents to other businesses. He and his wife lead short-term mission trips to Third World countries and provide financial support to team members who can't afford the trip costs.

Sandra is a floral designer for a local chain of flower shops. Each day, she was grieved to see flowers tossed away that were no longer considered fresh enough to sell to customers.

Yet, she knew from experience they would still last a few more days beyond the official expiration date. So she connected with a local church and started a flower ministry. Now she gathers the flowers that would otherwise be tossed, arranges them in beautiful bouquets, and personally delivers them to shut-ins, cancer patients, and the elderly.

John, Alan, and Sandra each had different gifts to share. As they trusted in God to meet their needs, they discovered that the gifts and blessings He provided were not theirs alone to hoard, but to steward well and let flow out freely to others (1 Corinthians 12:4–11; Matthew 25:29). The apostle Paul said, "If your gift is serving others, serve them well. If you are a teacher, teach well. If your gift is to encourage others, be encouraging. If it is giving, give generously. If God has given you leadership ability, take the responsibility seriously. And if you have a gift for showing kindness to others, do it gladly" (Romans 12:7–8). Further, he instructed Timothy, his protégé and pastor of the church at Ephesus, to tell the people to use their money to do good and be generous to those in need so that they may experience true life (1 Timothy 6:18–19).

Only God knows the ripple effect when His gifts and blessings flow out from within us like rivers of living water. Take John, as an example. John helps an unemployed father named Bill and shows him the love of Christ. He prays with him, encourages him, and coaches him through the job search process. Bill meets Jesus and his life is changed. Eventually, he starts a seekers' Bible study over the noon hour at his new job. He begins to minister and pray with Ann, a coworker struggling with a troubled teen. As a result, Ann seeks help for her son through a Christian residential program for chemically dependent teens. Her son graduates from the program and starts a street ministry for drug-addicted teens that eventually expands to other large cities. Soon thousands of teens are set free from drugs and receive Jesus as Lord. And the living waters flow on until it reaches the very ends of the earth (Acts 1:8)!

John, Alan, and Sandra can be compared to the Sea of Galilee, the main water source for all of Israel. The sea is really a freshwater lake fed by rain runoff from the mountains of Galilee. It is filled by the Jordan River that begins on the snowcapped peak of Mt. Hermon to the north and continues south to the Dead Sea. The river flows in and out so the water stays fresh and alive, similar to those who receive provision from God and continually give it away as God intended. Although the Dead Sea shares the same water supply, it has no outlet for the water that comes in. As a result, the water is salty, stale, bitter, and unable to sustain life. It is beautiful to look at, and the salt is worth a fortune, but the Dead Sea is dead—full of wealth but no life inside. It receives and it never gives.

Today, do you feel more like the Sea of Galilee or more like the Dead Sea? Perhaps you've received the Lord's living water, but you're keeping it all for yourself in a stagnant holding tank inside your heart. Everything may look beautiful on the outside, but on the inside, you are dying. Beloved, it's time to go back to the Source. Let Him restore your relationship and replenish your soul. When your relationship is right with God, His blessings will flow out from you in the same measure they flow in (Luke 6:38). If you show kindness to others as the Lord has shown kindness to you, He will guide you continually and water your life when you are dry. You will be like a well-watered garden or an ever-flowing spring (Isaiah 58:7, 10–11). Let nothing block the flow of living water within you.

Prayer

Lord, thank You for all the gifts and blessings You have poured into my life. Help me to be a good steward of my gifts and a generous giver. Thank You for the promise that the gifts I give to others will return to me in full—pressed down, shaken together to make room for more, running over, and poured into Your lap (Luke 6:38)!

Lord, I don't want to be like the Dead Sea. Forgive me for taking my eyes off of You, the Source of living water! Please show me the fears, emotions, selfishness, or anything else that has blocked the flow of living water. Lord, I return to You with a repentant heart. Thank You for unblocking the channel and replenishing my soul. Lord, I want to be like the Sea of Galilee! May rivers of living water flow continuously from within me.

Jehovah-Jireh: Ken's Story

"I want to talk to a pastor," Ken announced. He sat in his big leather chair, his feet on the ottoman with a crocheted afghan over his lap. His wife looked up from the book she was reading and stared at him from across the room. "Really?" she asked. He didn't answer. His eyes were fixed on the oversized window framing the panoramic view out the rear of the house. Rolling tree-covered hills filled the pink horizon as far as his eyes could see. They had carefully selected this lot. He wanted wide-open space to look at. They designed this room to relax and take in the view of the wildlife and the changing Minnesota seasons, each beautiful in its own right. It was early December and a fresh blanket of white snow covered the landscape. He knew he wouldn't see another spring through this window. He would probably not see Christmas.

He thought he had beaten the cancer. The intense headaches and blurred vision led to a diagnosis of grade IV glioblastoma. His daughter worked at a major cancer institute out east and arranged for the best doctors. He had surgery followed by radiation and chemo, and a year reprieve before it came back with a vengeance, its tentacles spreading wildly throughout his brain tissue and nervous system. Further surgery was out of the question and the last-ditch treatments they tried weren't worth the time and effort, not to mention the severe side effects. He was done.

He pondered this unexpected turn of events. He never thought it would end this way. All his life he had been a winner; a tough guy, a savvy deal maker. His business success was legendary among his friends and foes alike, and he could swing a golf club with the best of them. This house, a couple of vacation homes with all the toys, a corvette in the garage, and a huge retirement nest egg rounded out his goals. Working hard and smart and having a lot to show for it was proof of his success. Yes, he prided himself on being a winner. Now, for the first time in his life, he couldn't win. He couldn't beat this cancer. He couldn't beat death. He was surprised by how afraid he was to die.

His wife interrupted his thoughts. He didn't hear her come back into the room. She put her hand gently on his shoulder and said, "I called a friend. She knows a pastor. They're coming over." He nodded. *How odd.* He always believed religion was for weak people. People like him took life by the horns and wrestled it down. His fierce independence had been the key to his success. It was his life and he could only count on himself to make the most of it. *And here I am, asking for a pastor.* The irony of the situation was uncanny. *I can't think of that right now.* A thick, heavy fog slowly descended over his consciousness. It was the medication. Or maybe the cancer. He couldn't tell the difference anymore. His eyes grew heavy.

"Ken? You have company," his wife said. She was sitting on the edge of the ottoman touching his hand when he opened his eyes. "This is Pastor Jeanne," she said. When she was sure Ken had made the connection in his mind that he had asked for a pastor, she left the two alone. They exchanged a few words about their backgrounds and he told her a little about his diagnosis. She asked if he was in pain. Then Pastor Jeanne knelt on the floor in front of him, resting her arm on the ottoman and looking up into his face. "You've been through quite an ordeal," she said. "I'm so sorry you've had to suffer like this." "So am I," his said, voice cracking. They sat for a moment in silence. "God shed the first tear when you got this news," she said. He shrugged. Then she said, "How can I help?"

Ken took a deep breath and struggled to find the right words. "I worked hard. I tried to be a good person and provided a good life for my family," he said, as if it was very important for her to know this. "Yes, you have, Ken. You've been a good provider." She paused and asked, "What questions do you have for me?" The words spilled out. "I can't stand the pain anymore, but I'm so afraid to let go. What will happen to me?" She turned the question around. "What do you hope will happen?" His eyes fixed on hers. "I want to be free of this cancer and all this pain. I want to know my son is okay." His eyes misted and a tear ran down his mottled cheek. Probing further, she learned his little boy died at three. He gave her nothing more.

Then she said, "I know a place like that. A place where there is no more death or sorrow or crying or pain. Where your body is completely healed and restored and you will see your little boy again. God prepared a home for you in heaven."

He looked at her forlornly and said, "It's too late for me." "It's never too late," she said gently. "We all fall short, Ken. That's why He sent Jesus to pay the price for our mistakes. It's never about what we've done. It's all about what He did for us. He gave you a wonderful gift and is just waiting for you to accept it."

"How can I do that? How can I be sure?" he asked. "It's simple," she answered. "A simple 'sorry, thank You, please' is enough. You tell God you're sorry for your mistakes and for living life on your own terms. You thank Him for sending His Son to make things right and for dying on the cross for your mistakes. And you ask Jesus to please come into your heart and be your Savior."

Ken beat cancer that night, and two days later he beat death. Jehovah-Jireh provided the way. Heaven touched earth and took him home to the place where his real life had just begun. He traded all his wealth for streets of gold where he would be a winner forever.

Only One Thing

"There is only one thing worth being concerned about.
Mary has discovered it, and it will not be taken away from her."
LUKE 10:42

So much to do! So many people to feed! She bustled around making her dinner preparations. It was such an honor for Jesus and His disciples to visit her family in Bethany, a tiny village on the eastern slope of the Mount of Olives. They were on their way to Jerusalem for the Festival of Shelters after teaching throughout Galilee, and Martha welcomed them into her home. She had a reputation for her hospitality and this dinner had to be perfect.

While her guests rested from their travels, her sister, Mary, sat at the Lord's feet, listening to what He taught. But Martha continued to be distracted by the big dinner she was preparing. *Why doesn't she get up and help me? Can't she see what needs to be done? Our guests are hungry! What will they think if I can't get this meal on the table? This is Jesus, after all!* Her frustration mounted until she could stand it no longer. She came to Jesus and said, "Lord, doesn't it seem unfair to you that my sister just sits here while I do all the work? Tell her to come and help me."

But the Lord said to her, "My dear Martha, you are worried and upset over all these details! There is only one thing worth being concerned about. Mary has discovered it, and it will not be taken away from her." (Based on Luke 10:38–42.)

Martha and Mary both loved Jesus, but they served Him in different ways. Martha, the "responsible" older sister, was productive and task focused. She took the initiative to get things done to the point of making everyone else uncomfortable. Who else was going to get dinner on the table if she didn't? Mary, on the other hand, was doing *nothing* but sitting there! Martha thought her way of serving was better than Mary's, but in the process she was neglecting her guest, the Son of God. Her service had become self-serving and her heart cold and resentful. Jesus didn't condemn her for being concerned about the tasks at hand. He simply pointed out her priorities. There is a proper time to listen to Him and a proper time to do His work and right now, listening was a greater priority. Often, like Martha, our best intentions to serve Jesus can quickly deteriorate into a frenzy of busyness where our devotion to Him is lost in the shuffle. But Mary showed us that our worship and devotion always begin by spending time at His feet.

As the oldest, Martha was probably used to being in control. Hospitality was a social requirement in their culture and she obviously had it perfected. She had to do everything right and grew frustrated and felt sorry for herself that Jesus and no one else seemed to recognize her efforts. By the time she asked the Master to speak up for her, she had taken the task of preparing a perfect dinner all on her own shoulders and was concerned she wouldn't meet expectations. When we become Marthas, we can't bear the thought of dropping the ball and failing to meet expectations. Our identity has become defined by our performance and achievements instead of by the One whose child we are, the One who loves us even when we fall short— even when we drop the ball.

We all have to-do lists and expectations. Our days are packed full with details, responsibilities, and deadlines. How often do we rush out the door or jump into our work without giving God a second thought? Much of the fretting, worry, and mounting pressure to get it all done is because we failed to make room for Him. We have taken full responsibility for the tasks and details and left Him out completely. In our frenzy to keep all the balls in the air at once, our "dinner" might be perfect, but the Spirit of God isn't in it. We missed Him and all He wanted to teach us in the process.

God expects us to put forth our best effort, but we must always start with Him. Make room in your day to listen to the Master and spend time at His feet. In that place, you will always remember who and *whose* you are. As you trust Him, He will equip you to do the work He calls you to do (2 Timothy 3:17). He never expected you to do it on your own strength (Zechariah 4:6). When you keep Him in the center of your work, He will always make a way. Somehow, the dinner will come together and it will be delicious. Regardless of your tasks today, or how many details you must manage, only one thing matters. Mary found it. Will you?

Prayer

Oh Lord, so often I'm a Martha! I have the best intentions to include You in my day, to rest in Your presence and listen for Your voice. And then, something distracts me and I rush into my day without You. Forgive me, Lord, for worrying about the details, becoming upset, and losing my devotion to You in the frenzy of my busyness. I know when I make room to sit at Your feet, things always go smoother no matter how much is on my plate. Help me to keep You in the center of my work. I trust You to give me everything I need.

Lord, thank You that my identity is in You alone. I'm sorry for becoming worried, resentful, and feeling sorry for myself when others don't appreciate the work that I do. Forgive me for allowing performance and perfection to define me. I am Your child and You are a good, good Father, even when I fail and fall short. Lord, I want to be a Mary! I want to sit at Your feet regardless of the undone tasks around me. Teach me Your ways, Lord. I only need one thing. I only need You.

Hold Nothing Back

Looking at the man, Jesus felt genuine love for him. "There is still one thing you haven't done," he told him. "Go and sell all your possessions and give the money to the poor, and you will have treasure in heaven. Then come, follow me."

MARK 10:21

I must find Him. I must find the Teacher. I must know. There. . .there He is! The man ran to catch up. He had been a good man his entire life, taking meticulous effort to follow the law. Now, if this man was the promised Messiah, and he surely believed He was, then he must know for sure. *Have I done enough? Is there more?* Catching up and out of breath, he knelt before Him and asked the question that had been burning in his heart: "Good Teacher, what must I do to inherit eternal life?"

"Why do you call Me good?" Jesus asked attentively, knowing this man believed. "Only God is truly good. But to answer your question, you know the commandments: 'You must not murder. You must not commit adultery. You must not steal. You must not testify falsely. You must not cheat anyone. Honor your father and mother.'" Nodding his head and feeling very encouraged, the man replied, "Teacher, I've obeyed all these commandments since I was young."

But the Teacher's response caught him off guard. Looking at him with genuine love in His eyes, Jesus said, "There is still one thing you haven't done. Go and sell all your possessions and give the money to the poor, and you will have treasure in heaven. Then come, follow Me." An overwhelming sadness came over him. *But Teacher, I have many possessions.* Not knowing what else to say or do, he turned and walked away, head lowered and shoulders slumped, bewildered by the Teacher's impossible instructions.

Watching him leave, Jesus looked around and said to His disciples, "How hard it is for the rich to enter the Kingdom of God!" They looked at him amazed. Of all people, the rich should find no difficulty entering the Kingdom! But Jesus said again, "Dear children, it is very hard to enter the Kingdom of God. In fact, it is easier for a camel to go through the eye of a needle than for a rich person to enter the Kingdom of God!" Astounded, they asked, "Then who in the world can be saved?" Jesus looked at them intently and said, "Humanly speaking, it is impossible. But not with God. Everything is possible with God."

Always the bold one, Peter spoke up. "We've given up everything to follow You," he said. "Yes," Jesus replied, "and I assure you that everyone who has given up house or brothers or sisters or mother or father or children or property, for My sake and for the Good News, will receive now in return a hundred times as many houses, brothers, sisters, mothers, children, and property—along with persecution. And in the world to come that person will have eternal life. But many who are the greatest now will be least important then, and those who seem least important now will be the greatest then." (Based on Mark 10:17–31.)

The rich man who sought the Teacher for answers wanted assurance of eternal life. He had never broken any of the commandments and wanted to make sure he had done enough. But instead of something more to do, Jesus wanted him to submit his whole life and hold nothing back. He lovingly exposed the one thing he hadn't submitted to the Lord— his money and possessions. Wealth represented his pride of accomplishment and formed the basis for his identity and security. His possessions had become his idol—the one thing in his life he put before God. Ironically, in his deep desire to be obedient and follow all the commandments, he violated the first and greatest commandment: "You must not have any other god but me" and love Him "with all your heart, and all your soul, and all your mind" (Exodus 20:3–5; Matthew 22:37–38).

The disciples were astounded to hear it was harder for a rich person to enter the Kingdom than for a camel to pass through the eye of a needle. After all, the rich were highly revered in their culture. But as usual, Jesus turned their world upside down. Because of their money, power, and success, it was difficult for the rich to recognize their need for God. In their abundance, they could still lack the only thing that mattered: a saving relationship with Jesus. In contrast, Jesus assured them that those who gave up something valuable in this world for His sake would be rewarded many times over.

Jesus doesn't necessarily expect you to go sell all your possessions and give everything to the poor. But He does want to remove any barriers that stand in the way of your relationship with Him, especially the idols that take His place in your life. Imagine for a moment that He shows up at your doorstep this morning. You look into His loving eyes, scarcely able to breathe. Then, He gently places His nail-scarred hands on your shoulders and asks you to give Him your house—or your car, or your retirement account, or your job status, or your current level of income. Or perhaps your children, your family, your time, or your favorite hobby. What will you do? How you feel about His request might point to any barriers that keep you from full surrender. You can't trust Him with one part of your life, but hold back another. It all belongs to Him and it all came from His hands (Romans 11:36). And He wants you to hold on loosely and not let your blessings become your master. He wants you to hold nothing back.

Prayer

Lord, I'm grateful that Your gift of eternal life is not based on anything I do or how many commandments I obey, but on what You've done for me. You died so I could live in relationship with You forever. Help me to love You with all my heart, soul, and mind!

Lord, please point out anything that I am holding back from fully surrendering to You. Show me the idols of my heart. I don't want to worship anything or anyone but You. I want to put You first. Forgive me when I let the gifts You have given me take the place of the Giver. Help me to hold loosely, Lord. Help me to hold nothing back.

Not without God

Then Moses said, "If you don't personally go with us, don't make us leave this place."
EXODUS 33:15–16

Moses knew his assignment. God directed him to lead the Israelites home. But after the people disobeyed Him and worshipped the golden calf, God told Moses He wouldn't travel with them because they were a stubborn, unruly people. Sighing, he had to agree. Indeed, they were stubborn and unruly. And once again, he pleaded for mercy on their behalf. Then he continued his habit of spending time in the Tent of Meeting, consulting with God, worshipping, and resting in His presence.

Finally one day, he said to the Lord, "You have been telling me, 'Take these people up to the Promised Land.' But You haven't told me whom You will send with me. You have told me, 'I know you by name, and I look favorably on you.' If it is true that You look favorably on me, let me know Your ways so I may understand You more fully and continue to enjoy Your favor. And remember that this nation is Your very own people."

The Lord replied, "I will personally go with you, Moses, and I will give you rest—everything will be fine for you." Wanting assurance, Moses responded, "If You don't personally go with us, don't make us leave this place. How will anyone know that You look favorably on me—on me and on Your people—if You don't go with us? For Your presence among us sets your people and me apart from all other people on the earth." The Lord replied to Moses, "I will indeed do what you have asked, for I look favorably on you, and I know you by name." Emboldened, Moses responded, "Then show me Your glorious presence." The

Lord replied, "I will make all My goodness pass before you, and I will call out my name, Yahweh, before you. For I will show mercy to anyone I choose, and I will show compassion to anyone I choose." (Based on Exodus 33:1–19.)

Moses was not about to take a step forward without God's presence. He knew the power to complete his mission had to come from God, not his own human effort. He knew if God's favor went with him, He would provide everything he needed to complete the assignment. After God assured Moses that He would personally travel with him, Moses boldly asked God to see His manifest presence as proof. So God came down in a pillar of cloud and passed in front of Moses, revealing Himself as the merciful and gracious God (Exodus 34:5–6).

God's presence is everywhere. David said there was no place we could go to hide from Him (Psalm 139:7). His presence in the form of the Holy Spirit dwells within every believer (1 Corinthians 13:16). When we stay connected and aligned with His Spirit, He goes with us and provides everything we need to complete the work He calls us to do. He knows we can do nothing apart from Him (John 15:5).

For most of us, there is no shortage of tasks to complete. In addition to our families, work, and other activities, we have many opportunities to volunteer in our churches, communities, or schools. There are so many good things to do in the world; we can easily assume everything is *ours* to do. But God has a unique plan and purpose for each of us. Not everything is *your* assignment and God is not necessarily a part of everything that seems *good*. Moses prayed for God's presence to be with him before he moved forward and God said He would personally go with him and give him rest (Exodus 33:14). When we do good things for God without His presence and favor, we don't experience rest. We experience stress, anxiety, and burnout. Without Him in the middle, we have created a lot of commotion with no eternal significance (Hebrews 12:27).

Why do we find ourselves moving forward without God? Sometimes we know what He wants to do, but we get tired of waiting. So we jump ahead to make things happen on our own timetable, not unlike Sarah who grew tired of waiting for God's promised son and offered Abraham her slave Hagar (Genesis 16). Sometimes, we have poor boundaries. We just can't say no. We're focused on pleasing people instead of God (Galatians 1:10), or we're held captive by someone else's rules or expectations (Galatians 5:1). Sometimes, we take on more than our share to feel good about ourselves. Performance and achievement defines our identity and self-worth instead of knowing we are children of a good Father who loves us regardless of what we do.

Beloved, if God is a part of what you are doing, you will know it. His Spirit will speak to yours, and He will look upon you with favor. You will experience His peace, strength, wisdom, guidance, and protection even when your assignments are difficult. If you move forward without Him, you may feel as though you are pushing a boulder uphill. Your schedule is out of control, and you frantically try to hold everything together while the bottom falls out. Not every assignment from God will be quick and easy, but He will always give you rest—and everything will be fine for you. His yoke is easy and His burden is light (Matthew 11:30). Yes, go and complete your assignments, but not without God.

Prayer

Lord, I'm tired of pushing boulders uphill. I'm sorry for moving forward without You! Forgive me when people-pleasing and poor boundaries have taken me places You never intended for me to go. Help me to trust Your purposes and Your timing. Remind me that my identity and worth are in You alone, not in my achievements or my performance. Lord, I trade all my stress and anxiety for Your rest. I receive Your peace, Your strength, Your wisdom, Your guidance, and Your protection.

Lord, help me to stay aligned with Your Spirit, for without You, I can do nothing. I want to discern what You alone are calling me to do. I want to complete my God assignments on Your terms, not mine. Thank You for providing everything I need to do Your work. Look upon me with favor, Lord, and show me Your glorious presence! If You don't personally go with me, I don't want to leave this place!

Two Lost Brothers

*"Look, dear son, you have always stayed by me, and everything I have
is yours. We had to celebrate this happy day. For your brother was
dead and has come back to life! He was lost, but now he is found!"*
LUKE 15:31–32

*Will he let me come back? If he doesn't, I don't blame him. I really
blew it this time. I am so unworthy.* He was almost home. Things
just hadn't gone the way he planned when he set out on this
adventure. His pockets loaded with his portion of his father's
estate, he was finally free to make his own decisions and do what
he pleased. Or so he thought. The very things that drew him to
this faraway land had been his downfall. It didn't take long for
the wine, women, and wild parties to soak up all his money. And
who could anticipate the famine that made food so scare, he
could barely eat? He couldn't even find work, except with a local
farmer who sent him into his fields to feed his pigs. *Pigs!* He had
truly sunk to the depths of humiliation. And if that wasn't bad
enough, he was so hungry, even the pods he was feeding the pigs
looked good to him.

When no one helped him or seemed to care, he finally came
to his senses. *At home even the hired servants have food enough to
spare, and here I am dying of hunger!* So he decided to go home
to his father and beg for forgiveness. He knew he was no longer
worthy of being called his son, but he hoped he would at least
take him on as a hired servant. At least he would have food
to eat.

Almost there. Squinting his eyes, he thought he saw someone
in the distance. *Father? Is that you?* The figure started running
toward him. *It is! It's my father!* He was struck by his father's

apparent lack of concern for the undignified way his robe flapped in the wind exposing his legs as he closed the distance between them. But he was totally unprepared for what happened next. Filled with love and compassion, his father ran to him, threw his arms around him, and kissed him. As they embraced, the words and emotion poured out. "Father, I have sinned against both heaven and you and I am no longer worthy of being called your son," the younger man said with deep remorse.

Seeming to ignore his confession, his father shouted to his servants who had caught up with him, "Quick! Bring the finest robe in the house and put it on him. Get a ring for his finger and sandals for his feet. And kill the calf we have been fattening. We must celebrate with a feast, for this son of mine was dead and has now returned to life. He was lost, but now he is found." Humbled and too stunned to speak, the son headed toward the house to his welcome-home party—his father's embrace still holding him close. *Thank you, father. Thank you.*

Meanwhile, his older brother was in the fields working. When he returned home to music and dancing in the house, he learned his brother had returned safely and his father had killed the fattened calf to celebrate. Seething with anger, he refused to join the party. When his father begged him to come in, he replied, "All these years I've slaved for you and never once refused to do a single thing you told me to. And in all that time you never gave me even one young goat for a feast with my friends. Yet when this son of yours comes back after squandering your money on prostitutes, you celebrate by killing the fattened calf!" His father replied, "Look, dear son, you have always stayed by me, and everything I have is yours. We had to celebrate this happy day. For your brother was dead and has come back to life! He was lost, but now he is found!" (Based on Luke 15:11–32.)

In Jesus' story about the lost son, there were actually two lost sons. On the surface, the youngest did everything wrong and the oldest did everything right, yet they were both lost and destitute. Showing blatant disregard for his father's authority, the younger son rebelled and wanted to live as he pleased. He thought he would be able to survive on his own and make His own way. He made poor decisions and lost everything. He had to hit rock bottom before he could come back home and acknowledge his need for his father.

The older son believed he could make his own way, too, although his opposite approach was striving and hard work. He followed all the rules and worked hard to earn his rightful place. He sacrificed much for his father while his younger brother squandered everything, and he was bitter about the injustice of it all. For him, it was all about what he had done and what his younger brother failed to do. His self-righteousness stood in the way of celebrating his brother's return. He was a lot like the Pharisees who followed the rules and were resentful of sinners being welcomed into God's Kingdom. His arrogance and self-sufficiency made him just as lost as his brother.

We can learn much from these two brothers about our own relationship with our heavenly Father. We can be like the older brother and fail to see that God's grace cannot be earned through striving and hard work. He alone is the giver of all good gifts and the provider of everything we need (James 1:17). We can live in rebellion like the younger son and lose everything because we fail to steward well the gifts He has given us. We can choose a dwelling place far away from God and starve not only our body, but our soul and our spirit.

Have you been away from home too long? Feeling unworthy? Your Father is full of love and patience. He will give you plenty of opportunities to trust and depend on Him, but He won't force you to respond. If you've made mistakes, been out of touch for a while, or cut Him out of your climb to success, He can forgive your self-sufficiency and rebellion. His great love will run to embrace you and welcome you home, regardless of where you've been or how long you've been gone. A child was lost, but now is found! It's time to celebrate!

Prayer

Lord, thank You for your grace and mercy, for never leaving me or forsaking me, even when I leave You (Hebrews 13:5). Forgive me for the times I've rebelled against You—for the times I haven't been the best steward of the gifts You have given me, or I've been so focused on satisfying my own wants and desires, I've left You out of my decisions. I'm sorry for the times I've judged others for their lack of effort and forgotten that everything I have comes from Your hands. I can't earn Your favor by following rules and doing all the right things, while I disregard Your heart for the lost and broken around me.

Thank You that Your grace is a free gift so none can boast (Ephesians 2:9)! Your tender mercies start fresh every day (Lamentations 3:22–23). I want to come home, Lord. I want to run into Your loving embrace. I was lost, but now I'm found. Yes, Lord, it's a good day for a party.

His Place of Rest

For this good news—that God has prepared this rest—
has been announced to us just as it was to them. But it did
them no good because they didn't share the faith of those who
listened to God. For only we who believe can enter his rest.
HEBREWS 4:2–3

Caleb was bursting with excitement. They had *finally* arrived. God faithfully led them out of slavery, through the desolate wilderness, and to the very edge of the rich and fertile land He had promised to give their ancestors. Throughout the journey, He guided them, fed them, protected them, and performed amazing miracles. Caleb was thrilled to be one of the twelve scouts Moses sent to explore the land. Now, forty days later, he couldn't wait to give his report. Yes, it was all God had promised! The cluster of grapes they found was so large it took two of them to carry it on a pole between them!

Moses, Aaron, and the whole community waited anxiously to hear from the scouts. Sounds of wonder and amazement rose from the crowd when they saw the grapes and other fruit they brought back from the land. The crowd leaned in, eagerly waiting for good news when one of the scouts stepped forward to address Moses directly: "We entered the land you sent us to explore, and it is indeed a bountiful country—a land flowing with milk and honey. Here is the kind of fruit it produces," he said, pointing to the grapes. A hum of excitement rippled through the people. And then the scout continued. "But the people living there are powerful, and their towns are large and fortified. We even saw giants there, the descendants of Anak! The Amalekites live in the Negev, and the Hittites, Jebusites, and Amorites live in the hill country. The Canaanites live along the coast of the Mediterranean Sea and along the Jordan Valley."

A sound of alarm rose from the crowd. Sensing they were getting the wrong impression, Caleb quickly interjected to quiet the people. "Let's go at once to take the land," he said. "We can certainly conquer it!" But the other scouts disagreed: "We can't go up against them! They are stronger than we are!" Caleb was exasperated as this discouraging report spread among the people. Convinced they would be like grasshoppers next to the giants of the land, they wept aloud and cried all night. In a great chorus of protest against Moses and Aaron, they complained, "If only we had died in Egypt, or even here in the wilderness! Why is the Lord taking us to this country only to have us die in battle? Wouldn't it be better for us to return to Egypt?" In their despair, they wanted to choose a new leader to take them back to Egypt.

Hearing this, Moses and Aaron fell facedown on the ground before the whole community of Israel. Caleb along with Joshua, a fellow scout, tore their clothing. Making one last attempt to convince the people, they said, "The land we traveled through and explored is a wonderful land! And if the Lord is pleased with us, He will bring us safely into that land and give it to us. It is a rich land flowing with milk and honey. Do not rebel against the Lord, and don't be afraid of the people of the land. They are only helpless prey to us! They have no protection, but the Lord is with us! Don't be afraid of them!" But instead of changing their minds, the whole community began to talk about stoning Joshua and Caleb. (Based on Numbers 13–14:10.)

Caleb and Joshua were unsuccessful in convincing the Israelites to trust God's promise to bring them safely home, even though reaching the Promised Land had been their goal since leaving

Egypt. As a result of the people's unbelief, they wandered the desert for forty years until an entire generation died. Only Joshua and Caleb would enter the land because they trusted God would do what He promised (Numbers 14:20–34).

Your promised land is not the land of Canaan where Joshua would eventually lead the Israelites, but a new place of rest prepared just for you (Hebrews 4:6–10). We enter this place of rest through faith in Christ alone. It is both an eternal rest we receive on a new earth to come and a place of rest we can have today by trusting and obeying Him. It is found in the throne room of God where we can boldly enter and receive His grace and mercy (Hebrews 4:14–16). As a child of God, the same promises God gave to Abraham belong to you (Galatians 3:29). When you walk in His ways, He promises to bless you wherever you go, bless everything you do, and conquer your enemies when they attack you. He promises to provide for you from His rich treasury in the heavens and give you an abundance of good things in the land He is giving you (Deuteronomy 28:1–14).

Have you arrived in your promised land or are you still lingering around the border? Sometimes, like the Israelites, we can fail to enter our place of rest. We wander in the wilderness of doubt and uncertainty instead of receiving God's promises of provision and the abundance of good things that await us in our promised land. His promises did the Israelites no good because they didn't believe what God told them, even though He never once failed them. Beloved, since He did not spare His own Son, won't He graciously give you everything else (Romans 8:32)? Step out in faith and receive it. Trust Him to take care of the giants in your land. Because only we who believe can enter His place of rest.

Prayer

Lord, it's always so amazing to me that the Israelites would fail to trust You time and time again, even though You performed miracle after miracle and never once failed them. And then, I remember—I am so often just like them! Forgive me, Lord, when I allow my doubt and unbelief to keep me from receiving all You have promised me from Your rich treasury in the heavens!

Lord, I don't want to linger on the border anymore. Help me to trust and obey You. You are the God who never fails me, the God who conquers the giants in the land. Lord, I give You my fear. I step into my place of rest and receive the abundance of good things You have promised. Father, thank You for the gift of Your Son who made it possible for me to enter Your place of rest—today and forever.

Jehovah-Jireh: Amy's Story

It was exasperating. Can't they *see* what needs to be done? Details, so many details! Amy's job with a youth ministry organization was overwhelming at times. Managing the details was a juggling act, and she always had many balls in the air at once. But she had an eye for detail. *Someone* had to. Pulling off a ministry event for thousands of students was no small task. And, while managing the operations and logistics may not be her passion, it was her job. And she liked to think she was pretty good at it. Maybe even indispensable.

She served with an energetic and talented staff, all with a heart for pointing young people to Jesus. So why did it always feel like she was the only one who could see what needed to be done and when it needed to be done to keep things running smoothly? It was always the minutia, those little things that seemed insignificant to everyone else, but if forgotten or left undone, would derail an otherwise perfect event. So she would put her head down and keep moving fast—very, very fast. She was bound and determined that no balls would drop on her watch. And no one wanted to get in her way.

She had dreams and goals, too—a call to teach, a passion for prayer, a desire to help young people in crisis be healed and whole. But there was no time. There were always deadlines and details to manage: registrations, facilities, scheduling, logistics, marketing, parent communications, coordinating volunteers, and the never-ending list went on. She dreaded being the one at their team meetings to throw a wet blanket on all their creative ideas and plans. But someone had to point out all the underlying details and logistics it would require to make their plans a reality. Someone had to remind them of the time they tried it before and it didn't work. And that someone was always her. And she had a distinct feeling they didn't always appreciate her input. Well, she was willing to take that hit to keep things running smoothly, even if she was viewed as a naysayer. After all, it was her job. Even if her teammates didn't always appreciate her, she knew how much the organization *needed* her to keep all those balls in the air.

Until the day she learned they didn't need her after all. Leadership decided to eliminate her position. She was a valuable employee and there would be another role for her. But there would no longer be an operations manager. She was incredulous. *Who would take care of all the details?* Her job functions would be absorbed by the team, and the need for additional resources would be assessed. *How is this possible?* Even if they understood what needed to be done, they wouldn't have the time to do her job on top of their own! And there it was—proof they didn't value what she did. They didn't value her.

She spent the long weekend alone, trying to make sense out of what just happened. There was anger. But mostly tears. The wound cut deep. She cried out to God. *Lord, how could this happen? The ministry will fail without someone tending to all the details! How can I stay in this job? How can I work where I am not valued?* In the silence that followed, God began to gently speak to her. *You have lost your passion for Me.* At first she was stunned. *No, Lord! I work hard to serve You; to serve all the young people who need to know You!* Throughout the weekend, God began to reveal more. Her efforts to serve Him had deteriorated into a frenzy of busyness and her devotion to Him was lost in the details. And while she was wounded that they no longer needed her to do her job, she realized *she* no longer needed Him. She had taken it all on her own shoulders, striving for perfection, worrying about completing every detail, and making everyone uncomfortable in the process. Instead of being based on Christ, her identity and sense of value had subtly shifted to performance, achievement, and her job. *Trust Me, Amy.*

And she did. Today, she is working for the same ministry in a new position where she speaks regularly, ministers directly to students, and is developing her ministry and leadership gifting. She is still tending to details and logistics, but on a scope and schedule that allows time to spend at His feet. She is content and at peace. The team gradually adjusted to the transition somehow, without Amy holding all the balls in the air. She still cringes when she sees a ball drop, and she even rushes out to catch one once in a while. But she knows this is no longer her Kingdom assignment. She is working on trusting God to provide for the team. And she is amazed by Jehovah-Jireh, the God who provides, even when we don't know what we truly need.

Take Your Stand

"If we are thrown into the blazing furnace, the God whom we serve is able to save us. He will rescue us from your power, Your Majesty. But even if he doesn't, we want to make it clear to you, Your Majesty, that we will never serve your gods or worship the gold statue you have set up."
DANIEL 3:17–18

Shadrach, Meshach, and Abednego paused at the familiar sound of the horn, flute, zither, lyre, harp, pipes, and other musical instruments filling the air. It was their cue to stop everything they were doing and bow down to worship King Nebuchadnezzar's gold statue. *Never.* Again, they ignored the order. They were foreigners in this land and fully aware of the risk in this decision. After the king conquered Judah, he brought these three men and their friend Daniel back to Babylon as captives. The king was so impressed with their unusual aptitude for learning literature and science that he appointed them to his staff of advisors (Daniel 1:3–21). Eventually, Daniel became ruler over all of Babylon and appointed these three to be in charge of the province (Daniel 2:1–48). But the king had gone too far. His command to worship this ninety-foot-tall gold statue applied to *all* people, whatever their race or nation or language. And he had decreed that anyone refusing to obey would immediately be thrown into a blazing furnace.

Their disobedience did not go unnoticed. Appalled by their blatant disregard for the king's authority, some of the astrologers went directly to Nebuchadnezzar with their concern: "There are some Jews—Shadrach, Meshach, and Abednego—whom you have put in charge of the province of Babylon. They pay no attention to you, Your Majesty. They refuse to serve your gods and do not worship the gold statue you have set up." Upon hearing of their disobedience, the king was furious and ordered the three men to be brought before him. They were not surprised to be summoned. They fully expected it. *Never.* They stood silently and respectfully before the king waiting for him to speak.

"I will give you one more chance to bow down and worship the statue I have made when you hear the sound of the musical instruments," he threatened. "But if you refuse, you will be thrown immediately into the blazing furnace. And then what god will be able to rescue you from my power?" Confident and resolute, the men fixed their eyes on the king and replied, "If we are thrown into the blazing furnace, the God whom we serve is able to save us. He will rescue us from your power, Your Majesty. But *even if He doesn't,* Your Majesty can be sure that we will never serve your gods or worship the gold statue you have set up."

Filled with rage, Nebuchadnezzar commanded that the furnace be heated seven times hotter than usual and ordered some of the strongest men of his army to bind them up. Fully dressed, they stood in silence as the soldiers tightened the rope securely around them until they couldn't move and could barely breathe. A familiar peace descended upon each of them. *Our God will rescue us.* As the soldiers pushed them closer and into the roaring flames, they were surprised to see the same soldiers collapse and die instantly from the intense heat.

Now in the furnace, the flames immediately raged around them, engulfing them. *Our God will rescue us.* Incredulous, they watched as the flames licked their hair, clothes, and skin, but they felt no heat and no pain. The ropes that secured them fell away. There was a presence with them in the furnace, a presence like none other they had ever known. He was with them in the flames, dressed in a shimmering garment, bright as a flash of lightning. They stood in awestruck wonder, until they heard a familiar voice from outside the door shouting, "Shadrach, Meshach, and Abednego, servants of the Most High God, come out! Come here!" Stunned, Nebuchadnezzar witnessed four, not three, men walking around in the fire unbound and unharmed. *And the fourth looked like a god.*

The three men stepped out of the fire. Not a hair on their heads was singed, their clothing was not scorched, and they didn't even smell of smoke! Then Nebuchadnezzar said, "Praise to the God of Shadrach, Meshach, and Abednego! He sent his angel to rescue His servants who trusted in Him. They defied the king's command and were willing to die rather than serve or worship any god except their own God." (Based on Daniel 3:1–28.)

Standing with God isn't always easy. We often make excuses instead of doing the right thing. We compromise instead of trusting God to provide. We find ourselves worshipping at the wrong altars—the altar of success or the altar of convenience. We rationalize. After all, this is our *work* life. There are tasks to be done, deals to be made, deadlines to meet, and bosses to please. *Maybe I could bow down just this once, and then ask for forgiveness. What would it hurt? After all, God knows my heart. He knows what I really believe. Besides, this is a crisis! What choice do I have?* If we're not careful, our rationalizing can become a slippery slope of sin. Serving the god of money or the god of success begins to destroy your relationships. Doing something unsavory to increase your income or stature—or worse-case scenario, to save your job or business—becomes a little more acceptable. Before you know it, the one true God is just another god on the sidelines. He's no longer Lord of your life.

Shadrach, Meshach, and Abednego knew that to obey the king's order would be a direct violation of God's first commandment: "You must not have any other god but me" (Exodus 20:3). Unlike Nebuchadnezzar, they were not willing to add another god to their list of deities. They knew the one true God would provide a way, and their future was in His hands alone. When they landed in the fiery furnace as a result of their obedience, they trusted Him to come through, *even if He didn't*. They stood with God, no matter what the cost.

Can you take your stand with Jesus? You will always have opportunities to bow down and worship at the wrong altar. You can find shortcuts, temptations, and empty promises all around you. Even Jesus was pressured by Satan in the wilderness to compromise His destiny for an easier way (Matthew 4:1–11). When the pressure comes, remember He is a faithful God who provides for your every need (Philippians 4:19). He alone is worthy of your worship. He alone is worthy of your trust. Even if you are thrown into a blazing furnace, the God you serve is able to save you. No matter what the cost, take your stand.

Prayer

Heavenly Father, forgive me when my lack of trust in Your provision has led me to worship any other gods but You. Please forgive my excuses and rationalizations for not trusting You alone and for pushing You aside. You are the one true God who meets all my needs. You are worthy, Lord. Only You can save me from this slippery slope I'm on. Pull me up and set my feet on solid ground. I recognize Your rightful place as Lord of my life.

Lord, please give me spiritual eyes so I can see You and Your ways in all the temptations around me. Help me discern the things that are not of You. Help me do the right thing, even when I know I may land in the fiery furnace as a result! I trust You are able to save me. Help me to take my stand with You, no matter what the cost.

Shed Your Armor

"And everyone assembled here will know that the LORD *rescues his people, but not with sword and spear. This is the* LORD's *battle, and he will give you to us!"*

1 SAMUEL 17:47

Jack stared at the phone. The call would come soon. Months of hard work—networking, searching, and applying for jobs, following up on leads—it would soon be over. No more worries about house payments, car repairs, health insurance, or college tuition. He had done everything by the book—phone calls, long lunches, and relationships cultivated with internal contacts. "You're a shoo-in for this job," they all said. The phone rang. His heart beat faster as he exchanged pleasantries with his soon-to-be new boss. "I'm sorry, Jack, but we decided. . ." The rest of the conversation trailed off into the darkness as he tumbled into a pit of despair and disbelief. This cycle would repeat itself seven more times over the course of the next twelve months. With each defeat, the problem grew more and more insurmountable.

Three thousand years before, the Israelite army also faced an insurmountable problem: a Philistine giant named Goliath. For forty days he strutted back and forth, daring someone to come and fight him to determine which nation would be subject to the other. Seeing the Israelite army cower in fear, David was incensed. *How dare this pagan Philistine mock and curse the living God!* King Saul laughed when David offered to take care of the problem: "Don't be ridiculous! There's no way you can fight this Philistine and possibly win! You're only a boy!"

True, he was only a shepherd boy who cared for his father's sheep and goats. But he *knew* he could fight this giant and win: "When a lion or a bear comes to steal a lamb from the flock, I go after it with a club and rescue the lamb from its mouth. If the animal turns on me, I catch it by the jaw and club it to death. I have done this to both lions and bears, and I'll do it to this pagan Philistine, too, for he has defied the armies of the living God! The Lord who rescued me from the claws of the lion and the bear will rescue me from this Philistine!"

So the king agreed to let David fight. Saul tried giving him his own battle armor for protection, but David didn't like it and stripped it off. Fearlessly, the boy started across the valley to face the taunting giant armed with nothing but five smooth stones, a sling, a shepherd's staff, and all the confidence of a mighty king.

Goliath walked out to meet him, sneering in contempt and cursing in the names of his gods. "Am I a dog that you come at me with a stick?" the giant roared. "Come over here, and I'll give your flesh to the birds and wild animals!" Without so much as flinching, David replied, "You come to me with sword, spear, and javelin, but I come to you in the name of the Lord of Heaven's Armies—the God of the armies of Israel, whom you have defied. Today the Lord will conquer you, and I will kill you and cut off your head. And then I will give the dead bodies of your men to the birds and wild animals, and the whole world will know that there is a God in Israel! And everyone assembled here will know that the Lord rescues His people, but not with sword and spear. This is the Lord's battle and He will give you to us!"

David quickly ran out to meet Goliath as he moved closer to attack. Without hesitating, he reached into his shepherd's bag and took out a stone, hurled it with his sling, and hit the

Philistine in the forehead. The stone sank in, and Goliath stumbled and fell face down dead on the ground. (Based on 1 Samuel 17:16–49.)

David viewed his giant problem from God's perspective. He saw a mortal man, a pagan no less, defying the Lord of heaven's armies. Certainly, if God could save him from the claws of lions and bears, he had no doubt he could defeat this giant. And God was faithful. He used a slingshot, five stones, and the unwavering trust of a young shepherd boy to solve an insurmountable problem.

In the same way, everything changed for Jack when he started seeing his unemployment situation from God's point of view. He was no longer intimidated and discouraged when prospective employers said no. His job search was God's problem, not his. And he had the Lord of heaven's armies on his side. So he shed his armor. He stopped trusting his worldly weapons—the job prospects, the sophisticated interviewing techniques, the new suit, and the influential network of contacts—and put his trust in the living God who created the opportunities, the One who promised to meet all his needs (Philippians 4:19). Sure enough, God conquered his giant and he landed a good job.

As you face your giants today, are you clinging to your own resources, your own strength, and the weapons of this world, while all the time fearing it will never be enough? Beloved, no matter how insurmountable your problem, God doesn't need your arsenal of weapons to win. He just needs your trust. The Lord who rescues His people can give you the same courage and confidence He gave David. Your giant may come at you with sword, spear, and javelin, but you come in the name of the

Lord of heaven's armies. The battle is His, not yours. It's time to shed your armor.

Prayer

Lord, help me see my problem from Your perspective. You are bigger than my lack and insufficiency. You are so much greater than my current need. My giants do not intimidate You. Lord, You are a faithful God who rescues His people. Rescue me, Lord. I give You my fear. I give You this battle raging around me. It belongs to You.

Lord, forgive me for trusting in my own strength, my own resources, and the weapons of this world instead of You. Help me to trust in Your unlimited power and provision. Help me to shed my armor and face my giants in Your name alone. Lord, only You can save me (Psalm 33:20). The battle is Yours, not mine. Thank You, God. The Lord of heaven's armies is on my side!

Untouchable

"My God sent his angel to shut the lions' mouths so that they
would not hurt me, for I have been found innocent in his sight.
And I have not wronged you, Your Majesty."
DANIEL 6:22

Daniel knelt down as usual to pray in his upstairs room with its windows open toward Jerusalem. He cherished this time in God's presence. Three times a day, he prayed, gave thanks, and asked God for guidance. Worshipping God was his sanctuary, and he was not about to stop now.

Still on his knees, he sighed. He was well aware of the new law signed by King Darius. For the next thirty days any person who prayed to anyone, divine or human—except to the king would be thrown into the den of lions. He also knew the administrators and princes who had encouraged the king to sign the law. Oh, how they hated him! The king had chosen *him* of all people, a captive from Judah who had proven himself more capable than all the others, to supervise them and handle the king's affairs. They had no doubt heard of the king's plans to place him over the entire empire.

When he heard the king's soldiers coming to arrest him, he was not surprised. In the Medo-Persian empire, no law the king signed could be changed, even by the king himself. Of course, the conspirators knew that. The king grieved when he realized his predicament. He loved Daniel and found him to be faithful, honest, and responsible. He was angry at himself for signing the law and especially at the malicious men who had tricked him into it. But now he had no choice.

Daniel stood with Darius at the mouth of the den waiting

for the soldiers to throw him in. They stood in silence for a moment. He could see the pain in Darius's eyes. Then the king, seeing the peace on Daniel, said to him, "May your God, whom you serve so faithfully, rescue you." With that, the soldiers pushed Daniel into the den and placed the stone over the opening. The king sealed the stone with his own royal seal so that no one could rescue Daniel. Distraught, Darius returned to his palace and spent the night fasting. He refused his usual entertainment and couldn't sleep at all that night.

Daniel landed with a thud, his body hitting the cold, hard floor. While his eyes adjusted to the darkness, he heard the low, guttural sound of breathing as the lions moved stealthily toward him. One by one, they circled around him, snarling as they calculated their next move. He sat motionless, waiting for them to pounce, yet having a strange sense that they wouldn't. And then, he saw it. A tall, shimmering figure appeared, radiating a brilliant glow over Daniel and the lions. To his amazement, instead of tearing into his flesh, the lions purred like kittens and lay down around him. *Oh my God, my God!* Leaning against them on the floor, he marveled at God's faithfulness and waited for morning to come.

Very early the next morning, the king got up and hurried out to the lions' den. When he got there, he called out in anguish, "Daniel, servant of the living God! Was your God, whom you serve so faithfully, able to rescue you from the lions?" Daniel answered, "Long live the king! My God sent His angel to shut the lions' mouths so that they would not hurt me, for I have been found innocent in His sight. And I have not wronged you, Your Majesty." The king was overjoyed and ordered that Daniel be lifted from the den. Not a scratch was found on him, for he had trusted in his God. Then the king gave orders to arrest the men who had accused Daniel and had them thrown into the lions' den. And he sent a message to the people of every race and nation and language throughout the world that they should tremble with fear before the God of Daniel. (Based on Daniel 6:1–26.)

Daniel had a disciplined prayer life that others couldn't help but notice. Darius even referred to Daniel's God as "the God whom you worship continually." He was convinced of God's power because Daniel was faithful and God rescued him. Daniel didn't let anything, not even the threat of death, interfere with his prayer life. Intimacy with God was his lifeline, and it sustained him throughout captivity. Even though he had a good relationship with Darius, he knew the king couldn't help him escape the lions' den. Only God could provide the guidance and strength he desperately needed. He knew God would save him because he *knew* God. The deep, personal relationship he had cultivated through a lifestyle of prayer and worship assured him of God's faithfulness, regardless of his circumstances.

Beloved, the same God who rescued Daniel can deliver you from your lions' den. Consistent prayer and devotion is your lifeline to His power and His presence. As your relationship grows deeper and you grow in your knowledge of Him, you will come to understand the confident hope He has given you and the incredible greatness of His power (Ephesians 1:17–19). You will learn to trust Him more and more, regardless of the challenges you face. The evil one can't touch you, for God's Son holds you securely (1 John 5:18). No evil can conquer you, because you have made the Lord your refuge and the Most High your shelter (Psalm 91:9–10). All because you know the One who closes the mouths of the lions. In Him, you are untouchable.

Prayer

Lord, there are so many distractions that keep me from spending time in Your presence. Forgive me for letting the stresses of this world interfere with my prayer life. I want You to be known as the "God I worship continually," the God who rescues me from all my trials and troubles.

You are my lifeline, Lord. You are the source of all good things and everything I need. I want to know You. I want to know Your nature and understand the incredible greatness of Your power and the confident hope I have in You. You are my refuge, Lord. You alone are my protection. In whatever circumstances I face today, help me to trust in the One who closes the mouth of lions. In You, I am untouchable.

Open the Gate

Suddenly, there was a bright light in the cell, and an angel of the Lord stood before Peter. The angel struck him on the side to awaken him and said, "Quick! Get up!" And the chains fell off his wrists.
ACTS 12:7

Sixteen soldiers stood guard, four squads of four soldiers each. Peter looked down at the shackles that held him captive. *Lord, after all we've been through, does it end like this?* His thoughts trailed off. After the resurrection, they had received the Holy Spirit, just as the Lord promised. He preached boldly by the Spirit's power and watched thousands respond to the Gospel message. But the religious leaders continued in their relentless persecution. Many believers fled from Jerusalem after Stephen's brutal death (Acts 7). Now, King Herod Agrippa was the latest pawn in their efforts to destroy the rapidly growing Church. He was grandson of Herod the Great and the Romans had appointed him to rule over most of Palestine. Hoping to solidify his position, he began to persecute some of the believers. Tears stung his eyes. The king had John's brother James killed with a sword. When he saw how much this pleased the Jewish people, he also arrested Peter. He would bring him out for public trial after the Passover. Peter breathed deeply. *They will execute me, like Stephen, James, and all the others.* As disturbing as the thought was, a deep peace fell over him.

He sat on the damp floor, his back against the hard stone wall, each wrist fastened by a chain to the wrist of a solder on each side. The others stood guard at the prison gate. His eyelids grew heavy. It was no use fighting sleep now. Morning would soon come, then the trial. Sleep overtook him. Deep in slumber, he felt something touch him on the side. Startled, he jolted awake, his eyes squinting as a bright light filled the cell. *Am I dreaming? Is it. . .is it an angel?* Indeed it was! "Quick! Get up!" the angel said. Before Peter could react, the chains fell off his wrists. He jumped up to his feet as the angel gave further instructions: "Get dressed and put on your sandals." And he did. "Now put on your coat and follow me," the angel ordered.

Following the angel, he left the cell. *This must be a vision. It can't be really happening. It's impossible.* But he kept following anyway, close at the angel's heels. They passed by sleeping guards at the first and second guard posts and came to the iron gate leading to the city. *Trapped.* But just as he concluded there was no way out, the gate opened for them all by itself. They passed through and started walking down the street when the angel suddenly left him.

It's really true! The Lord has sent his angel to save me! He hurried to the home of Mary, the mother of John Mark, where many followers were gathered for prayer. *God answered their prayers!* Excited, he knocked at the door in the gate. "It's me, Peter!" he said urgently. Rhoda, a servant girl, came to open it. When she recognized Peter's voice, she was so overjoyed that, instead of opening the door, she ran back inside and told everyone, "Peter is standing at the door!" "You're out of your mind!" they said. When she insisted, they decided, "It must be his angel."

Exasperated, he kept knocking. *Open the door, friends!* When they realized the knocking would persist until they investigated, they finally opened the door. And there stood Peter. They stared in stunned silence before breaking out in celebration. He motioned for them to quiet down and told them how the Lord had led him out of prison. "Tell James and the other brothers what happened," he said. And then he left them. At dawn there was a great commotion among the soldiers about what had happened to Peter. Herod Agrippa ordered a thorough search for him. When he couldn't be found, Herod interrogated the guards and sentenced them to death. (Based on Acts 12:1–19.)

Peter's ministry was going well. The Church was expanding, and with the Holy Spirit's power, they were unstoppable. And then the persecution came. Stephen was stoned to death, the believers scattered, James was executed, and Peter was next. In spite of this sudden turn of events, Peter slept soundly. He fully expected to be executed in the morning like James. He wasn't wringing his hands in anguish. Jesus warned there would be troubles, but He told them to take heart because He had overcome the world (John 16:33). He warned there would be persecution for those who believed in Him and followed His teaching (Matthew 10:16–33). By now, Peter had a Kingdom perspective. He simply trusted God would provide.

Sometimes we, too, experience the unexpected. The business is thriving, the job is going well, the family is all getting along, and everything is going according to plan. You're sure you are in His will and His favor is on you. Then, without warning, the bottom falls out: a serious accident, a life-threatening diagnosis, a broken trust, a devastating loss. Suddenly you find yourself in shackles, unable to move, unsure how to escape, unsure what will happen next, and wondering if this is the end of the road. Or perhaps you wake up one day and realize you've been living in a prison all along. Unresolved wounding, disappointments, and lost dreams have kept you locked in the chains of your past; unforgiveness and bitterness have held you captive in a self-made prison of sin.

While Peter was locked in chains, fellow believers prayed

earnestly for him, and suddenly, everything changed. God moved in response to their fervent prayers and set Peter free. In the same way, prayers of intercession by others on your behalf can change everything. God can intervene suddenly because what is humanly impossible is always possible with God. He can provide an escape, even if you find yourself in a prison of your own making. Coming to Him with a humble and repentant heart can bring forth sudden breakthrough and freedom from the strongholds that keep you in shackles and prevent you from receiving all He has planned for you.

Peter had a divine destiny. Jesus said He would build His Church upon him and all the powers of hell would not conquer it (Matthew 16:18). No one would frustrate His purpose for Peter. Beloved, God will always fulfill His purposes in you. He has a plan for your life and you have a destiny to fulfill (Jeremiah 29:11). He will rescue you from the hands of your enemies so you can serve Him without fear (Luke 1:74). No one can stand in His way. You may be in shackles, but the Lord can open the gate.

Prayer

Lord, I'm in prison. I feel the cold, damp floor and the shackles that bind my wrists. I'm tired, Lord, and I want to be free. Help me get past my past. Show me who I need to forgive, and reveal anything I need to confess to You that keeps me in bondage. Forgive me, Lord! Replace the lies I have believed with the truth of who You are and who I am in You. You are a good God, and I am Your beloved child! I trust You to provide an escape!

Thank You for Your plan and purpose for my life. Nothing can steal my destiny! Please send intercessors to pray for my breakthrough when I am too weak to pray. May their earnest prayers move Your heart, Lord. There may be troubles in this life, but I fully expect You to rescue me. Loosen the shackles and open the gate!

The Lord Lives!

The LORD lives! Praise to my Rock!
May the God of my salvation be exalted!
PSALM 18:46

King David was one of the greatest men in the Old Testament, well known as a shepherd, giant-killer, poet, mighty warrior, and ancestor of Jesus. He was also a skilled musician who played the harp for King Saul (1 Samuel 16:23) and brought music to the Lord's Temple (1 Chronicles 25). King Saul was so pleased with David's musical talent and military successes that he took David into his home and treated him as a son. But when he realized God had anointed David to replace him as king, his insane jealousy drove him into a murderous rage. David and his loyal followers fled for their lives, hiding in caves in Philistine territory for years before Saul died and David finally became king of Judah in his place.

David wrote many of the Psalms during his time of hiding from a jealous King Saul. He learned to praise and thank God, even while his enemies pursued him relentlessly. He most likely wrote Psalm 18 (also found in 2 Samuel 22:1–51) toward the end of his life as he looked back with gratitude on God's glorious works. We can learn much about God's faithfulness and be encouraged in our own time of need by reflecting on David's song of gratitude.

David begins by describing God and His character and how he had experienced Him in his life. God proved to be his strength—rock, fortress, protector, shield, place of safety, and the power that saved him (Psalm 18:1–2). He describes the intensity of his need and how the Lord heard his desperate cries for help:

"The ropes of death entangled me; floods of destruction swept over me. The grave wrapped its ropes around me; death laid a trap in my path. But in my distress I cried out to the LORD; yes, I prayed to my God for help. He heard me from his sanctuary; my cry to him reached his ears" (Psalm 18:4–6).

He vividly describes how God responded to his cry with such power and anger at his enemies that the earth trembled, the mountains shook, and the foundations of the earth were laid bare at the blast of His breath: "Smoke poured from his nostrils; fierce flames leaped from his mouth. Glowing coals blazed forth from him. He opened the heavens and came down; dark storm clouds were beneath his feet. Mounted on a mighty angelic being, he flew, soaring on the wings of the wind. He shrouded himself in darkness, veiling his approach with dark rain clouds. Thick clouds shielded the brightness around him and rained down hail and burning coals. The LORD thundered from heaven; the voice of the Most High resounded amid the hail and burning coals. He shot his arrows and scattered his enemies; great bolts of lightning flashed, and they were confused" (Psalm 18:8–14). Then, He reached down and rescued David, drawing him out of deep waters and leading him to a place of safety (Psalm 18:16–19).

David fought many battles over the course of his life, but he knew it was God who prepared him, strengthened him, and gave him victory in every one: "He trains my hands for battle; he strengthens my arm to draw a bronze bow. You have given me your shield of victory. Your right hand supports me; your help has made me great. You have made a wide path for my feet to keep them from slipping. I chased my enemies and caught them; I did not stop until they were conquered. I struck them down so they could not get up; they fell beneath my feet. You have armed me with strength for the battle; you have subdued my enemies under my feet" (Psalm 18:34–39).

Even after David sinned against Uriah the Hittite by taking his wife, Bathsheba, and sending him to the front lines to be killed, he was quick to confess his sin and his repentance was genuine. He knew he stood blameless before God (Psalm 18:23). God forgave him and showed him mercy and even referred to him as a "man after my own heart" (Acts 13:22). David never took God's forgiveness lightly or His blessing for granted.

Beloved, you can know the same God King David knew—the Rock that can't be moved, the Fortress, who is your place of safety—your Shield, your Strength, and the Stronghold that holds you high above the enemies' reach. His is the same God who hears your desperate cries for help when the floods of destruction sweep over you. He is the One who opens the heavens and comes down, soaring on the wings of the wind, shooting His arrows and scattering your enemies with great bolts of flashing lightning. He is the same God who reaches down to rescue you from deep waters, the same One who prepares and strengthens you and stands by you through every battle you will ever face. He is the living God, the One who gives you victory! Praise to your Rock! May the God of your salvation be exalted!

Prayer

Lord, the only way I can be delivered from the trouble that surrounds me is to call on You for help and strength. You are my provider, the One who meets my every need. Lord, today may my desperate cries for help reach Your ears! Open the heavens and come down to earth! Come, Lord, come! Let the brilliance of Your presence break through the dark clouds! Come with such power that the foundations of the earth are laid bare! Shoot Your arrows and scatter my enemies, Lord! Hold me safe beyond their reach!

Lord, thank You for being the lamp that lights up my darkness. You have made a wide path for my feet to keep me from slipping (Psalm 18:36). I can trust You will either draw me out of the deep water or carry me through whatever trial I face. In Your strength I can crush any army and scale any wall (Psalm 18:28–29). Thank You for standing beside me, teaching me, and giving me the strength to be victorious. Indeed, the Lord lives! Blessed be my Rock!

Jehovah-Jireh: Shelly's Story

Shelly was delighted to be pregnant again. Her nineteen-month-old boy needed a little brother or sister, and two years between them would be the ideal plan. A little girl would round out the perfect family of four, but she really didn't care. She was grateful for whatever the Lord provided, whether a boy or girl. She already loved the little one and prayed every day for a healthy, happy baby.

Everything was going as well as expected at the beginning of the pregnancy. And then it wasn't. She knew something was wrong. She had severe morning sickness with her first pregnancy, but this time was different. This time it was worse. Instead of gaining, she was losing weight. And as a petite size 0 who barely topped one hundred pounds, there were no pounds to spare.

At first she attributed the weight loss to the morning sickness. It would get better, she thought. But it didn't get better. She was pregnant and *losing* weight instead of gaining weight. Even the food she could hold down went right through her. Her doctor had tests run on her GI tract: parasites, bacterial infections, endoscopy, colonoscopy, and more. All negative. Since she had a history of allergies to pollens, grasses, and other outdoor allergens, it was time for her allergist to test for food allergies.

One by one, each test came back. Each call from the allergist was more bad news. There was finally an explanation for her symptoms. She had true immune system hypersensitivity to all fruits, all vegetables, nuts, and most grains. All healthy foods, foods unborn babies needed to flourish. Her immune system mistakenly identified these foods as dangerous, triggering a protective response. When she ate these foods, her body would send out antibodies that released chemicals to defend against it. In essence, her body was rejecting the very food she and her unborn child needed to live and making her very sick in the process.

Shelly was devastated. The only foods her body wouldn't reject were meat, dairy, rice, and chocolate. And she could barely hold those down. Every meal was a struggle. She spent many days doubled up on the couch in pain, battling stomach cramps, diarrhea, and vomiting. She had a toddler to care for and an unborn child to nourish. By now, she knew she was carrying a little girl, but worry about her diet and how it was impacting the baby's development threatened to steal her joy. At twenty-three weeks pregnant, the scale read ninety-six pounds, six pounds under her normal weight. Her obstetrician was at a loss for what to do. Her allergist had nothing to offer but *future* research. *And how does that help now?* Shelly, the planner, had no plan. *Oh God, help me.*

Shelly's family shared in her desperation and felt an urgent need to take immediate action. They reached out to an extended family member who worked at a world-renowned medical center located in another part of the state. God opened a door and she was able to cut through some red tape to connect Shelly with a leading allergist there. She allowed herself to feel hopeful. Upon examining her, the doctor made an unsettling observation: "Women in your compromised nutritional condition do not typically carry babies to full term." She chose to view this statement positively. She was now nearly six months pregnant, two-thirds of the way home.

Since her digestive tract could not absorb essential nutrients, he sent her home with pre-digested food packets, the same substance used for tube feeding, only she was to *drink* it four times a day. It was brutal. He also wanted to reset her immune system with a series of allergy injections over the next few years. But there was a catch. The drug was approved for severe asthma, and not food allergies. And it was very, very expensive. He would submit the prescription for approval to her insurance company and hope for the best.

She had reason for hope. An emergency food plan, even though she had to choke it down and pray it stayed there. And a long-term plan to address the food allergies. The possibility of eating again someday like a regular person was almost too good to be true. Now, all they could do is wait. And, what about the baby? Had her development suffered? *Lord, is she okay?* Her obstetrician would run tests to learn more.

In the meantime, Shelly continued to choke down the liquid "food" while waiting for approval from insurance. Every time the baby moved brought her relief. She talked to her. She talked to God. She prayed. Her family prayed. They prayed that the tests would show a normal baby in spite of the conditions. They prayed the approval would come from the insurance company. Each passing day brought her closer to the due date. In spite of the emergency food, she was growing weaker and the scale didn't move. Without the allergy shots, what would she eat? Where would she find the strength and sustenance to care for her children and live her life?

The news finally came. The insurance company

denied payment. She was devastated. The doctor provided additional information to plead her case. But they denied it a second time. And a third. As a last resort, he appealed to the pharmaceutical company to provide the drug free of charge, a program for those who couldn't afford the exorbitant out-of-pocket cost. More waiting. Shelly and her husband were desperate. He was afraid. He felt like he was watching his pregnant wife starve to death. And she was sick, weak, thin, and nearing the end of hope. A family member rushed to the home to pray and encourage her, and prayer ministers and intercessors from their church continued to pray.

And God heard their cries. A few days later, she received some good news. The drug company approved her request for assistance. Arrangements were made for her local allergist to receive the drug and begin administering the injections as soon as possible. And the best news of all: Test results showed a healthy baby. Her fetal development had not been impacted by her mother's malnourishment.

Four years have passed. Shelly is still receiving her allergy shots, complements of the drug company. Little by little, her immune system has corrected itself, and she is able to enjoy most of the healthy foods her body once rejected. Her little girl is healthy, vibrant, and happy. Strangely, her favorite food is meat, one of the only foods her mother could hold down during her pregnancy. Mealtime prayers have a whole new meaning for Shelly and her family. They give thanks every day to Jehovah-Jireh, the God who provides.

A New Beginning

Throw off your old sinful nature and your former way of life,
which is corrupted by lust and deception. Instead, let the Spirit
renew your thoughts and attitudes. Put on your new nature,
created to be like God—truly righteous and holy.

EPHESIANS 4:22–24

She stumbled trying to keep up with the teachers of religious law and the Pharisees who were dragging her down the street. Some people stopped and stared when they heard the commotion. They knew. There was only one explanation for a woman to be in trouble this early in the morning. There was no use fighting them. They caught her leaving her lover's home. She tried to sneak out unnoticed, but they had been watching. And now, what would they do to her? Would they have her stoned according to the Law of Moses? Would the whole town witness her punishment? *I will die in my shame.*

She soon realized they were taking her to the Temple. As soon as the religious leaders dragged her inside, she saw Him. He was sitting with the crowd that had gathered, teaching them. When He heard them enter, He stopped speaking and turned toward them, His eyes fixing on hers. He held her gaze for a moment. He knew. They shoved her in front of the crowd for all to see as she stumbled to her knees.

Turning to Jesus, one of the religious leaders spoke: "Teacher, this woman was caught in the act of adultery. The law of Moses says to stone her. What do You say?" Jesus knew they were trying to trap Him into saying something they could use against Him. He paused for a moment, and then He stooped down and began to write in the dust with His finger. *Who are these men to accuse? Their sins are many.* But they kept demanding an answer: "Teacher, what do You say?" She cowered in a heap on the floor, aware of the crowd's staring, but more aware of the Teacher. His eyes had penetrated her soul. Gentle eyes—eyes of love and compassion like she had never known before. He stood up again and said, "All right, but let the one who has never sinned throw the first stone!" Then he stooped down again and wrote in the dust. He continued to list the sins of those who accused her. He knew.

Stunned, she watched her accusers slip away one by one, beginning with the oldest, until only she and Jesus were left in the middle of the crowd. Then He stood up again and said to her, "Where are your accusers? Didn't even one of them condemn you?" "No, Lord," she said, looking up into the eyes of love itself. And Jesus said to her, "Neither do I. Go and sin no more." (Based on John 8:1–11.)

As they did so often, the religious leaders were trying to trap Jesus. While it may have violated Jewish law not to stone *both* the woman and the man involved for their transgression (Deuteronomy 22:22), only the Roman government was permitted to carry out an execution (John 18:31). Jesus rose above their trap and responded with mercy toward this woman. He made it clear that not one of these religious men was without sin and, as a result, they were no different from the woman they wanted to punish. The God of compassion and forgiveness, the only One with authority to judge, provided her a way out of sin and shame. He gave her a fresh start, a new beginning.

He can do the same for you. There is no condemnation in Him, regardless of what you have done (Romans 8:1). He died for every mistake you ever made and every mistake you will ever make. When you gave your life to Him, you became a brand-new person (2 Corinthians 5:17). He wiped your slate clean *forever* and will never again remember your sin (Hebrews 10:17). In fact, He removed your transgressions from you as far as the east is from the west (Psalm 103:11–12). You now stand holy and blameless before Him, a child of God, without a single fault (Colossians 1:22).

Yes, sometimes you fall short and engage in wrong behavior, even though God has already made you righteous through Christ's blood. Even the apostle Paul acknowledged he had not reached perfection. But he kept working toward the day when he would be all that Christ saved him for and all that God created him to be (Philippians 3:12). What a comfort to know His tender mercies start fresh every day (Lamentations 3:23)! A simple confession and He is faithful to forgive you and purify you from all unrighteousness (1 John 1:9).

Beloved, today your accusers may be demanding justice for your shortcomings. You may be surrounded by a crowd who wants you to pay for your mistakes. But, He has already paid the price in full. He provided you a way out of your sin and shame. He gave you a fresh start today, and He does not condemn you. Throw off your former way of life and go and sin no more. Let the Spirit renew your thoughts and attitudes. Put on your new nature, created to be like God—truly righteous and holy. For today is a new beginning.

Prayer

Lord, as hard as I might try, You know I am far from perfect. Yet, perfection is what You see when You look at me through the lens of Christ's love. But I still make mistakes, sometimes really big mistakes! In spite of the accusing words of others when I fall short, thank You that in You, there is no condemnation. You are faithful to forgive and provide a way out of all my messes. Thank You for separating me from my sin, as far away as the east is from the west!

Lord, thank You that the old me died with You on the cross. Help me to put on my new nature, created to be righteous and holy just like You. Help me to go and sin no more. I want to become the person You see when You look at me. Thank You for new beginnings!

Redeeming Love

Then the women of the town said to Naomi, "Praise the LORD,
who has now provided a redeemer for your family!
May this child be famous in Israel."
RUTH 4:14

She was a widow in this foreign land. And as a widow and daughter-in-law of a widow, Ruth had to work and make her way. A severe famine had forced her husband's family to leave Bethlehem and settle in Moab, her homeland. But her father-in-law, Elimelech, died soon after, and later his two sons. When his widow, Naomi, returned to Israel after the famine, she insisted her Moabite daughters-in-law return to their own families and remarry. But Ruth refused and promised, "Wherever you go, I will go; wherever you live, I will live. Your people will be my people, and your God will be my God."

Today, she worked in the harvest fields. The law permitted the poor to gather leftover grain for food, and she was not too proud to join them. She worked hard all morning with only a few minutes' rest in the shelter. As she followed the harvesters picking up the grain they spilled on the ground, she noticed a distinguished-looking man had arrived and was speaking to the foreman. *He must be the owner of this field.* She overheard from the others his name was Boaz. As they motioned in her direction, she could tell they were talking about her.

The distinguished man started walking in her direction. *What does he want?* As he drew close, she smoothed her skirt and looked up at him, waiting for him speak. "Listen, my daughter," he said. "Stay right here with us when you gather grain; don't go to any other fields. Stay right behind the young women working in my field. See which part of the field they are harvesting and then follow them. I have warned the young men not to treat you roughly. And when you are thirsty, help yourself to the water they have drawn from the well."

Relieved and overwhelmed with gratitude, she fell at his feet. "What have I done to deserve such kindness?" she asked. "I am only a foreigner." "Yes, I know," he replied. "But I also know about everything you have done for your mother-in-law since the death of your husband. I have heard how you left your father and mother and your own land to live here among complete strangers. May the LORD, the God of Israel, under whose wings you have come to take refuge, reward you fully for what you have done."

"I hope I continue to please you, sir," she replied. "You have comforted me by speaking so kindly to me, even though I am not one of your workers." At mealtime he invited her to eat with his harvesters and allowed her to keep the leftovers. When she went back to work again, she noticed there was more grain leftover to gather, as if the harvesters in front of her were dropping it on purpose! She gathered barley there all day, and when she beat out the grain that evening, it filled an entire basket. She hurried back into town, excited to give the grain to Naomi along with her lunch leftovers.

When Naomi learned the field Ruth worked was owned by Boaz, she was ecstatic. "May the LORD bless him! He is showing his kindness to us as well as to your dead husband. That man is one of our closest relatives, one of our family redeemers." So Ruth worked alongside the women in Boaz's fields gathering grain until the end of the barley harvest and through the wheat harvest in early summer, all the while living with her mother-in-law. (Based on Ruth 1–2.)

The story of Naomi and Ruth is one of God's goodness and grace in the midst of desperate circumstances. As widows, neither woman had a means of financial support. Ruth was a woman of strong character who was not too proud to admit her need and work hard to meet it. She took advantage of Israel's welfare program, the law that allowed the poor to glean grain in the fields for food (Leviticus 23:22). Her love, kindness, hard work, and faithfulness did not go unnoticed by her mother-in-law, the townspeople, or her new God.

The Lord's guidance led Ruth to the field that belonged to Boaz, a relative of her father-in-law, Elimelech. According to Jewish law, inheritance could only be passed on to a son or the nearest male relative. The nearest male relative to a deceased husband could become the family redeemer by buying the property and marrying the widow so the inheritance could stay in the family. Without a redeemer, a widow like Ruth would live in poverty the rest of her life. A kind and generous man, Boaz became the family redeemer. He married Ruth and she bore him a son named Obed, who gave Naomi great joy and cared for her in her old age. He was the father of Jesse and the grandfather of King David, from whom Jesus the Messiah would descend (Ruth 4:13–17).

Naomi and Ruth came to Bethlehem as poor widows, but God's hand of protection was on them. He honored Ruth's obedience and kindness to her mother-in-law. Her loyalty and character in their time of need brought them both great blessing, even greater than seven sons (Ruth 4:15). In the same way, God can bring great blessing out of your desperate need. Don't hesitate to ask for help or take a humble step into the "harvest field." Let your difficult times be opportunities to strengthen your character and deepen your faith. He is always watching. He always has plans and purposes beyond your understanding. And His love always redeems.

Prayer

Lord, thank You that Your hand is upon me, no matter how dire my circumstances might be. Show me where my pride or disdain for certain jobs or tasks may have kept me from my harvest field of blessing. Forgive me, Lord! Help me to work faithfully unto You at whatever job You give me to do (Colossians 3:23–24). Thank You for Your strength and guidance. As I take refuge under Your wings, I trust that my faithful obedience, hard work, love, and kindness can open new doors of opportunity!

Lord, use these difficult circumstances in my work or finances to strengthen my character and deepen my faith in You. Help me to trust You, even when I can't see what You're doing. You are my ultimate Redeemer, Lord. Your plans for my life are beyond anything I can ask or imagine. I can trust You to care for me throughout my life and even into my old age. Thank You for Your redeeming love.

A Love Overflowing

"I tell you, her sins—and they are many—have been forgiven,
so she has shown me much love. But a person who is
forgiven little shows only little love."
LUKE 7:47

For years, Julie believed she had no other choice. She had to make a living. Of course, most of the money went to *him*. She never thought it was possible to get out. Who would hire her for a real, honest job at this stage of the game? No, she was in too deep. She never felt worthy of anything else. And then she had a child. Everything changed when her little boy was born. A friend of a friend knew of a program that could help her get out of "the life." They provided housing and gave her a new start. She was in a program learning life skills, receiving counseling, and exploring career paths and training programs. *A real career!* It was beyond anything she had dreamed possible.

The program connected her with a church where she received spiritual care and support and learned about Jesus—how He didn't condemn her, and died so she could have a new life. She had never been to church before, and all her preconceived ideas about "church people" were shattered. Instead of judging her, they were helping her heal from her broken past and get to the root of her feelings of unworthiness. She had no car, but a kind woman from the church was providing transportation back and forth to meetings and even taking care of her son. She had never known people could be so kind and expect nothing in return. They didn't even know her, but it didn't seem to matter. For the first time in her life, she had hope. She was overwhelmed with love and gratitude for this God who pulled her out of the pit and showed her a love she had never known existed.

Two thousand years ago, there was another woman who was overwhelmed with love for her Savior. She heard Jesus was eating dinner at the home of one of the Pharisees. *I must see Him.* She was an uninvited guest, but she didn't care. She entered the house unannounced, ignoring their stares. In her arms she carried a beautiful alabaster jar filled with expensive perfume. *For Him.* And there He was, lying on a couch at the table, His head propped up on one elbow with His feet stretched out behind Him. Overwhelmed with emotion, she quickly dropped down on her knees behind Him. Tears spilled out of her eyes and fell on His feet as she wiped them off with her hair. Over and over, she kissed His feet and anointed them with perfume intermingling with her tears of gratitude.

She felt the disgusted look on the host's face. His name was Simon and he knew exactly who she was. Yes, she was an immoral woman, and she was touching Him. Jesus seemed to know, too. "Simon," he said to the Pharisee, "I have something to say to you." And He told him this story: "A man loaned money to two people—500 pieces of silver to one and 50 pieces to the other. But neither of them could repay him, so he kindly forgave them both, canceling their debts. Who do you suppose loved him more after that?"

Simon answered, "I suppose the one for whom he canceled the larger debt." "That's right," Jesus said. Then he turned to the woman and said to Simon, "Look at this woman kneeling here. When I entered your home, you didn't offer Me water to wash the dust from my feet, but she has washed them with her tears and wiped them with her hair. You didn't greet Me with a kiss, but from the time I first came in, she has not stopped kissing

My feet. You neglected the courtesy of olive oil to anoint My head, but she has anointed My feet with rare perfume. I tell you, her sins—and they are many—have been forgiven, so she has shown Me much love. But a person who is forgiven little shows only little love." He said to the woman, "Your sins are forgiven. Go in peace." (Based on Luke 7:36–50.)

Both of these women lived and worked in a prison of shame they thought was inescapable. But all along, God had a plan for their escape. He put people in Julie's life who demonstrated His love and compassion in tangible ways and opened the doors to a new life in Him. The woman who lavished tears, expensive perfume, and kisses on Jesus's feet received the forgiveness she desperately longed for, all while His host scorned and failed to show Him the most basic level of hospitality and respect. Both women were being held in lowly and degrading positions of servitude. But Jesus pulled all women up into a place of fellowship and service showing they were equal in the eyes of God (Luke 8:2–3). Both women understood the depth of their transgressions and the magnitude of His forgiveness and their transformed lives. The only way they could respond to His love and mercy was to love Him back with the same love they had so graciously received (1 John 4:19).

Sometimes the pressure to make ends meet or to put food on the table for ourselves or loved ones leads us to make choices that do not honor God and His ways. It could be something seemingly small, like occasionally withholding cash from a tax return, or a major lifestyle choice that has locked you in a prison of sin and shame with no way of escape. Regardless of your transgressions, no mistake can escape His outstretched arms of forgiveness. Nothing can ever separate you from His love that is revealed in Christ (Romans 8:38–39). And when you receive the gift of a transformed life, you can't help but lavish tears of gratitude on the feet of your Savior. You can't help but respond with a love overflowing.

Prayer

I have gone astray, Lord. I have not fully trusted in Your provision, and I have made my own way. I am in a prison of shame and see no way out, but I know You always have an escape plan. Help me, Lord! Please put people in my path who will lead me to an open door. Thank You that Your outstretched arms of forgiveness cover all my transgressions.

I need a new start, Lord. Thank You for pulling me out of the pit of despair and hopelessness and setting my feet on solid ground (Psalm 40:1–3). Today, I sit in Your presence and receive Your forgiveness and mercy. Thank You that nothing I can do will ever separate me from Your love. Words cannot express my gratefulness, Lord! My love overflows like perfumed kisses on Your feet.

Give It All to Him

My heart rejoices in the LORD! The LORD has made me strong.
1 SAMUEL 2:1

She picked at her food. She couldn't eat. She was *still* childless and so tired of the constant reminders. The shame and desperate unmet longing to carry a child in her womb and hold him at her breast were simply too much to bear. So she got up and went to the Tabernacle to pray. Eli the priest was sitting at his customary place beside the entrance. She was in deep anguish, crying bitterly as she prayed to the LORD. And she made this vow: "O LORD of Heaven's Armies, if You will look upon my sorrow and answer my prayer and give me a son, then I will give him back to You. He will be Yours for his entire lifetime, and as a sign that he has been dedicated to the LORD, his hair will never be cut."

As she rocked back and forth on her knees, her mouth was moving but she was praying under her breath. She felt the priest watching her. "Must you come here drunk?" he demanded. "Throw away your wine!" *Oh Lord, he thinks I have been drinking!* "Oh no, sir!" she replied. "I haven't been drinking wine or anything stronger. But I am very discouraged, and I was pouring out my heart to the Lord and praying out of great anguish and sorrow." "In that case," Eli said, "go in peace! May the God of Israel grant the request you have asked of Him." Lifted by his words, she exclaimed, "Oh thank you, sir!" And she got up and left and began to eat again, for she was no longer sad. After worship the next morning, she and her family returned home to Ramah.

In due time, the Lord remembered her plea. Smiling

and deeply grateful, she placed her hand on her belly and felt the child moving in her womb. She had never known such contentment. When she gave birth to her son, she named him Samuel, meaning, "I asked the Lord for him." The long-awaited child brought her great joy and, at the same time, great remorse when she remembered her promise. *I must return him to the Lord.* But somehow, in the midst of her sorrow, joy would rise up and she knew all would be well.

And then, it was time. The child was three years old and no longer nursing. She and her husband Elkanah returned to Shiloh. *Yes, Lord, it's time.* Hannah took Samuel by his little hand and entered the Tabernacle. Approaching the priest, she asked. "Sir, do you remember me?" *Yes, he does.* She continued, "I am the very woman who stood here several years ago praying to the Lord. I asked the Lord to give me this boy and He has granted my request. Now I am giving him to the Lord, and he will belong to the Lord his whole life." And once again, she prayed. "My heart rejoices in the Lord! The Lord has made me strong!"

She held her child close, her heart breaking. *Good-bye, little one. The Lord will keep you now.* She turned and left him, and they headed back home to Ramah. But each year she made a small coat for him and brought it to him when she came with her husband to Shiloh. And when they left, Eli would bless them and say, "May the Lord give you other children to take the place of this one you gave to the Lord." And the Lord did. Hannah gave birth to three more sons and two daughters. And Samuel assisted Eli the priest and grew up strong in the presence of the Lord. (Based on 1 Samuel 1–2:21.)

In Old Testament culture, a childless woman like Hannah was considered a failure and a social embarrassment. Children were part of the social and economic structure, both working for the family and caring for their parents in old age. Hannah was so depressed about her situation that she was physically ill and unable to eat. Her deep longing to cradle a child in her arms, the stigma of her barrenness, and torments of others pushed her into a place of desperation. She brought her problem before the Lord and poured out her raw emotions. She was so desperate for Him to move in her life that she offered Him the very thing she wanted most. She knew a child would be a gift from God, so she wasn't offering to give him *up*, but to give him *back*. Her commitment was costly, but she followed through. Samuel was not only the Lord's helper, but he become a prophet of God, a renowned leader, and the greatest judge in Israel (1 Samuel 3:19–20). In return for her obedience, God blessed Hannah with more children.

If you are a parent, the thought of giving a three-year-old child to the leaders of your church probably seems ludicrous. But we can all relate to barrenness, can't we? There are times when nothing appears to be bearing fruit in our work or relationships. The sales don't come, the job opportunities fall through, or maybe you have spent years longing for a spouse or perhaps even a child. And all your best efforts have given birth to nothing but emptiness. At times like this, we can reach a point of such anguish that our unfulfilled desires literally make us sick (Proverbs 13:12).

Beloved, prayer opens the way. It is your antidote for discouragement. Cry out to the Lord like Hannah. Give Him your anguish and raw emotions. Give Him the problem, along with everything else you have. It all belongs to Him. And then go in peace, trusting He will provide. His timing is not always yours, but His timing is always perfect. He knows the desires of your heart and exactly what you need. He is making plans and preparations behind the scenes that you may never fully understand. And He can bless you beyond measure when you give it all to Him.

Prayer

Oh Lord, I am barren! I have been holding on to this desperate desire far too long. My best efforts have given birth to nothing! I am in deep anguish and filled with sorrow. My hope has been deferred time and time again, and my heart is truly sick! Take it, Lord. Take this desire You placed in my heart. I give it back to You.

Lord, every good and perfect gift comes from You alone (James 1:7). I give it all back. I surrender every part of my life to You. Every blessing—my family, job, abilities, possessions, hopes, and dreams— it all belongs to You. Use it all for Your glory. My heart rejoices, Lord! Let my life be a testimony to Your power, Your greatness, and Your goodness. Yes, Lord. I give it all to You. Oh, how You have blessed me!

For Such a Time

"Who knows if perhaps you were made queen for just such a time as this?"
ESTHER 4:14

Janelle was the director of communications for a major health care organization. The job was fast-paced, high-paying, and all-consuming. And it wasn't working for her anymore. When she started talking about leaving to start a consulting practice, family and friends were stunned. Her job made up two-thirds of the family's income; she had a college-bound child and another one on his heels. Who in their right mind walks away from a job like this? But it was also taking a huge toll on her family, her health, and her quality of life. She knew in her heart quitting was the only way out. When she gave her notice, the boss who recruited her felt betrayed. *God, I hope Your hand is in this. It makes no sense otherwise!*

Things were rough at first. The family had to adapt to a significant drop in income while she got her business established. There were many days of uncertainty, even questioning whether she had heard God correctly. Eventually, former colleagues who had left the company for other opportunities began engaging her services. God restored her relationship with her former employer and they became her best client. She had more positive influence with the people she worked with as an outside consultant than she ever did as an employee. Best of all, her flexible schedule allowed for more time with family and better life balance. As final confirmation of her decision, she was elected to the board in her rapidly growing suburban church, where her leadership gifting played a key role in helping the church impact thousands of lives for the Kingdom. *Yes, Lord. Your hand of favor is surely upon me.*

Janelle moved from a place of security into a place of divine influence, but not without significant risk. In a decision that made no worldly sense, she discerned what God was doing and responded in faith to His favor. God's favor is simply His desire to show undeserved kindness toward us. He does so because He is a good Father who loves His children. Favor is a part of God's grace, a free gift we receive through faith in His Son (Ephesians 2:8). We activate our faith by believing God is who He says He is, and He will do what He promises to do. Through His grace, we find favor with God and man to receive everything Jesus died for and the power to do what He calls us to do. His favor is manifested through the blessings we receive and our opportunities to bless others.

While God's favor is available to all, He has His own agenda (1 Samuel 2:7). We can see from scripture how many great heroes of faith found favor to accomplish His purposes. For example, Ruth found favor with Boaz and became the great-grandmother of David (Ruth 2–4). Samuel grew in favor with the Lord and people and became the greatest judge in Israel (1 Samuel 2:26). Mary found favor with God and became the mother of Jesus (Luke 1:28–30). Jesus grew in wisdom, stature, and favor with God and became the Savior of the entire world (Luke 2:52; 1 John 4:14). The apostles had favor with both God and man and grew the church (Acts 2:47).

A perfect example of God's favor is found in the story of Esther, a beautiful young Jewish woman. King Xerxes, who reigned over the vast Medo-Persian empire from his fortress in Susa, made Esther his queen after banishing Queen Vashti for refusing to obey him. Esther and her cousin Mordecai, an official in the king's government, were part of the Jewish minority that was deported from Judah one hundred years earlier, although the king was unaware of Esther's Jewish heritage.

Haman, the king's second in command, despised Mordecai for refusing to bow down in reverence to him. Determined to destroy Mordecai and all the Jews in the land, he tricked the king into issuing an edict condemning all the Jews to death. When Esther received Mordecai's request to go beg the king for mercy and plead for her people, she sent him this message: "All the king's officials and even the people in the provinces know that anyone who appears before the king in his inner court without being invited is doomed to die unless the king holds out his gold scepter. And the king has not called for me to come to him for thirty days." And Mordecai responded, "Don't think for a moment that because you're in the palace you will escape when all other Jews are killed. If you keep quiet at a time like this, deliverance and relief for the Jews will arise from some other place, but you and your relatives will die. Who knows if perhaps you were made queen for just such a time as this?" So Esther agreed to see the king, even though it was against the law: "If I must die, then I am willing to die."

Three days later, when Esther put on her royal robes and entered the palace, she found favor with the king. Not only did he reach out his scepter, but he offered to grant her request, even if she were to ask for half the kingdom. Esther exposed Haman's plot to destroy her and her people. The outraged king had Haman executed, appointed Mordecai to take his place, and granted the Jews protection throughout the land. (Based on Esther 2–8.)

God lifted Esther out of obscurity, placed her in a position of influence, and her courage saved an entire nation. She believed God was in control and followed His guidance, despite the risk. He did the same for Janelle, and He can do the same for you. He may be placing you in a particular job, position, or location and giving you influence to accomplish His purposes. This is not the time to cower in fear and doubt, but to move forward in confidence, trusting He will give you favor in everything according to His will. When you know His hand of favor has brought you this far, you can trust He will continue to bless you and others through your obedience. Whether you are called to impact your home, workplace, community, or the world—perhaps it was for such a time as this.

Prayer

Lord, give me the courage to step into my favor. Help me to follow Your guidance in spite of the risks I see all around me. I give You all my doubt and fear. Your gracious favor is all I need, Lord. I know Your power works best in my weakness (2 Corinthians 12:9). Help me to trust in Your plans and purposes for my life, even when the call You have placed on my heart makes no worldly sense.

Lord, help me to move forward in confidence, trusting Your hand of favor is upon me to accomplish all You have called me to do. You are my King, Lord. Reach out Your scepter and show me Your favor! I believe You have placed me here, for such a time as this!

Jehovah-Jireh: Kelsey's Story

She knew it was a mistake. People with her paltry salary as a church worker had no business buying property. But they told her she could afford it. Even her parents were behind it. Historically, in her city, a townhouse like this would appreciate rapidly. She could sell in a few years when she got married and use the equity for a generous down payment on a house. So she reluctantly borrowed the money for a first mortgage and took out a second mortgage for the down payment. "It's done all the time," they assured her again. The interest rate was fixed at a low rate for the first few years, but she would be out of the property before the variable rate kicked in. And there was no need to pay down principle. By paying "interest only," her payments would be low enough to qualify for the loans. "It's done all the time," they assured her. She took in a roommate to help manage the cash flow and take the edge off her unsettled spirit. And then she sat back and waited for the property values to rise.

Yes, it was a great plan. Until it wasn't so great. Property values *didn't* rise. They tumbled. She had purchased her property at the peak before the housing market crashed. And now, she was "underwater" in her mortgage. Not just underwater. She was drowning. She owed thousands of dollars more than her property was worth in the current market.

With each passing year, she felt more and more chained to this property. The unknowns tormented her. How would she make the payments if interest rates increased? If she ever got married and had to sell, how would she cover the difference in the value of the townhouse and the amount she owed? No lender would let her refinance to lock in a fixed rate as long as she was underwater. She knew that because she'd checked. Many times she checked. She didn't qualify for the government programs designed to help underwater homeowners because she didn't have the right kind of mortgage. Fortunately, the interest rates stayed at rock bottom so she could still afford the interest-only payments when her roommate left and got married. She was even able to turn the spare bedroom into an art studio. Her modest pay raises and selling some of her paintings made it possible to meet expenses without finding another roommate. Time passed, and she kept hoping for a housing boom that would make the problem go away. *Even if God brought a spouse into her life, couldn't she rent out the property until the market bounced back?* It was always in the back of her mind, the threat of increased payments she would be unable to afford and property she couldn't sell.

And then it happened. She received notices from both lenders on the same day. Her new monthly payments included higher interest plus the principle she was now required to pay. She quickly calculated her monthly expenses. Her take-home pay covered the new payments plus utilities and homeowners fees. Nothing left to buy food, gas, and basic necessities. Nothing left to live. She panicked. Again, she reached out to the lenders. There was nothing they could do. She didn't qualify for the government programs that helped people like her. Instead, the lenders she spoke to advised her to default on her current mortgage and go through foreclosure. "It's done all the time," they said. "Your credit rating will bounce back in a few years." *Unacceptable.* She always paid her bills on time and had a stellar credit rating. She was not about to go down that path. So instead, she cancelled her gym membership. She cancelled her cable television. She stopped going to Starbucks. She advertised for a roommate, knowing she would be giving up her beloved art studio. And then she prayed. She gave the problem to God because there was nothing more she could do.

And God answered. While searching her lender's website for some information, she discovered she could apply for her mortgage to be "restructured." *No one had told her about this option.* She completed the lengthy, arduous paperwork and submitted it to the lender. Praise Jesus, she qualified for help after all! Her lender agreed to restructure the mortgage for a longer term and lower fixed rate. And then, without even requesting it, her second mortgage lender reached out with the same offer! Her combined payments were now lower than before, she is reducing her debt, her interest rates are fixed, and it all cost her nothing.

Kelsey still hopes to sell someday. She is trusting the market values will catch up to her debt. In the meantime, she reinstated her gym membership. She still drinks Starbucks. And she still paints in the studio she gave back to God—all glory to Jehovah-Jireh: the God who provides!

Get It Back

And the LORD told him, "Yes, go after them.
You will surely recover everything that was taken from you!"
1 SAMUEL 30:8

Sam was let go from a high profile sales position with an international company when his position was eliminated. They no longer needed his services. Now if the shock and anguish of a sudden job loss wasn't enough, there was more. About the time of his termination and by the terms of his plan, he figured they owed him a significant bonus. But when he contacted several people within the company to lay out his case, they ignored his claim. Apparently, they felt no obligation to pay out the bonus. Sam disagreed, and so did several people he trusted and respected. One of them recommended a trustworthy attorney specializing in employment law.

Sam and his wife agonized over filing a lawsuit. The company was huge and had unlimited resources at their disposal. They could easily take the case as far as they wanted. But Sam was one man with very limited resources. Would it be worth the time, money, and emotional stress? Could he win? What were his chances? How long would it take? One year? Two? More? But mostly, what would God have him do? Should a Christian be suing in the first place? He was grateful for his years of employment and had already forgiven his employer. Were there other ways to seek God for justice?

One morning, while he and his wife were praying over the decision and doing their morning Bible study over coffee, the phone rang. It was a prayer partner from church. "I was reading the story of David when the Amalekites burned Ziklag to the ground," he said. "God kept bringing you into my mind." Sam felt God might be answering his prayers for guidance and immediately went to the reference in his Bible.

Now according to the story, when Saul was pursuing David to kill him, he sought refuge with the Philistines. He pretended allegiance to King Achish who was so impressed with David and his reputation, he let him and his men settle in the town of Ziklag. When war broke out with Israel, God used the suspicions of the other Philistine commanders to protect David from having to fight against his own countrymen. King Achish had no choice but to send him back to Ziklag.

When David and his men arrived home, they found that the Amalekites had burned the town to the ground and carried off the women and children. When they saw the ruins and realized what had happened to their families, they wept bitterly. David's men were so distraught about losing their sons and daughters that they turned on him and began to talk of stoning him. But David found strength in the LORD and sought His counsel: "Should I chase after this band of raiders? Will I catch them?" And the LORD told him, "Yes, go after them. You will surely recover everything that was taken from you!"

So David and his men set out to recover all that the Amalekite raiders had stolen. Along the way they found an Egyptian slave, abandoned by his Amalekite master because he was sick. As they nursed him back to health, David learned that he had been returning with the group of raiders who had just burned Ziklag. "Will you lead me to this band of raiders?" David asked. The young man replied, "If you take an oath in God's name that you will not kill me or give me back to my master, then I will guide you to them."

So the Egyptian led David to their camp, where they found

the Amalekites spread out across the fields, eating, drinking, and dancing with joy because of the vast amount of plunder they had taken. David and his men rushed in among them. They fought them from dusk until the evening of the next day and none of them got away, except four hundred young men who fled on camels. David got back everything. Nothing was missing: small or great, son or daughter, nor anything else the Amalekites had taken. (Based on 1 Samuel 27; 29; 30:1–19.)

Sam was encouraged. While David's men turned on him looking for someone to blame, David took action by seeking God for a solution. He asked the Lord for direction; the Lord said, "Go," and David obeyed. Along the way, God provided guidance through an Egyptian slave who led them directly to the raiders. So Sam asked the Lord for direction: "Lord, You know I have forgiven my former employer. I've turned this problem over to You. You are a God of justice, Lord. Should I go after what I rightfully earned? Should I take action against this company to recover what was taken from me? Was the attorney recommendation from a friend and this phone call part of Your guidance?"

Sam felt God leading him to at least meet with the attorney. He soon discovered he was indeed trustworthy. He was a believer who agreed Sam had a strong case. And then God removed a huge barrier. The attorney offered to take the case on contingency, meaning he would take a percentage of any settlement that resulted to pay for his services. So Sam moved forward with his suit. It took some time, and it wasn't an easy undertaking. Sam had prayer cover, and he often prayed for his former employer during the process. Eventually, God gave him favor with the judge and the case was settled.

Beloved, you may not find yourself in the throes of a lawsuit, but you live in a world where the enemy still prowls around like a roaring lion looking for some victim to destroy (1 Peter 5:8). He still kills, steals, and destroys, even though Jesus came to give you abundant life and provide for your every need (John 10:10; Philippians 4:19). Has the enemy stolen your health, your job, your finances, your relationships, or any other provision that came from His hands? Maybe it's time to go get it back.

Prayer

Lord, thank You for being my provider. Help me to be thankful for all You have given me, even when it seems like I'm losing it all! Lord, You are my guide and my counselor. Holy Spirit, lead me in every part of my life (Galatians 5:25). Give me Your divine wisdom and show me Your ways (1 Corinthians 2:12–13). Teach me to do Your will and lead me forward on firm footing (Psalm 143:10).

Lord, You know exactly what the enemy has stolen from me. I chose to forgive those who wronged me, and I release this loss into Your hands of justice. I know only You can heal the pain this loss has caused me. And I know I can trust You to redeem what I lost. Lord, if there is any action I need to take to recover what the enemy stole from me, please show me. Help me hear Your voice. Draw me into Your Word. Bring godly people into my life who can confirm Your will and guide me along the way. Lord, show me if it's time to get it back!

Where Were You?

"Where were you when I laid the foundations of the earth? Tell me, if you know so much."
Job 38:4

Jason was a thirty-three-year-old commercial airline pilot living the dream. As an avid motorcyclist, flight instructor, and first-degree black belt, he was in excellent health and worked out regularly. All his hard work was starting to pay off. He was active in his church and community and just about to get engaged, settle down, and raise a family. And then, overnight, everything changed.

He woke up with a pounding headache. It felt like a terrible hangover, but he hadn't had a single drink the day before. The next day was no better. Or the next. At first he attributed it to jet lag. He tired easily and, even though he rested, he kept growing weaker. Then came the other symptoms: digestive problems, swollen glands, fatigue, malaise, muscle stiffness, and more.

He sought answers from medical doctors, chiropractors, naturopathic doctors, nutritionists, dentists, physical therapists, and infectious disease specialists, including some well-renowned specialists. They found nothing major. Several doctors attempted to steer him toward a mental health diagnosis, but he knew his body, and he knew he wasn't crazy. Thirty-six doctors and two years later, he finally got the answer from a Lyme literate medical doctor (LLMD). He tested positive for several tick-borne infections. Diagnosis: "chronic" or "late stage" Lyme disease.

Recovery would not be short or easy, they said. There is no standard protocol to fight this disease and key stakeholders in the health care system don't agree on the scope and nature of the problem. Research is underfunded, and most doctors are clueless about how to diagnose it, let alone treat it. Two years later, Jason is still fighting. His days are filled with a long list of all-consuming medical and alternative treatments. He continues to ride a roller coaster of symptoms. Some have resolved completely, while others still linger. The severity and unpredictability of his symptoms along with the scope and side effects of the treatments forced him to temporarily hang up his wings. His employer has been gracious, and some of his friends and family have shown compassion. Others have simply disappeared. Many have offered unhelpful counsel. Jason thinks of everything he has lost—his health, his career, his relationships—and he ponders his unknown future. He can't help but cry out to God in the silence: *Where are You? Why did this happen? God, I want my life back.*

Job wanted to know, too. *God, where are You?* He was a righteous man who loved God and lived a life of wealth and prestige. And then, everything changed. His livestock, servants, farmhands, home, and all his children were suddenly destroyed (Job 1:13–19). After everything was stripped away, he was struck with a dreadful case of boils from head to foot (Job 2:7). As he sat in ashes, scraping his skin with broken pottery, his wife told him to curse God and die (Job 2:8–9).

In his deep anguish, Job did not curse God. Instead, he cursed the day of his birth. He believed it was better never to be born than to be forsaken by Him (Job 3). *God, where are You?* Why had He allowed Job's world to crumble despite his right living? His friends came to comfort him, but instead, they offered less than helpful advice. One insisted that sin had caused his suffering and urged him to repent (Job 4–5; 15; 22). Another accused him of not admitting his sin (Job 8; 18; 25). A third friend thought Job deserved to suffer even more (Job 11; 20).

Finally, the Lord spoke to him from a mighty whirlwind. He didn't give Job any answers. Instead, He asked a series of questions Job couldn't possibly answer. *Where were you when I laid the foundations of the earth?* (Job 38:4). *Have you ever commanded the morning to appear and caused the dawn to rise in the east?* (Job 38:12). *Who sends the rain that satisfies the parched ground and makes the tender grass spring up?* (Job 38:27). Job realized his limited human mind couldn't even grasp the wonder of God's physical creation. How could he possibly understand God's mind and character? He responded by humbling himself before God (Job 42:1–6). After Job prayed for his friends, God restored his fortunes, giving him twice as much as he had before (Job 42:10–16).

Job let his need to know *why* consume him until God made it perfectly clear. It's better to know God than to know why. He didn't owe Job an explanation (Job 38–41). Job learned that when everything else was stripped away, God is all he ever had. Like Job, Jason may never understand why everything was stripped away. He may never know what the Lord is thinking or be wise enough to give Him advice (Romans 11:33–34). In the midst of his loss, all he can do is cling to God's promise to give him a future and a hope (Jeremiah 29:11). Because God is all he ever had and, everything he lost belongs to Him, God alone has the power to heal and restore. In the meantime, Jason has dedicated his time to help others afflicted by this devastating disease through advocacy and education.

Today, you might be wondering, "Why did this happen to me?" You can desperately search for answers. You can even curse God and give up. *Where is this God who provides?* Beloved, He is right there with you. He would never leave you or forsake you

(Hebrews 13:5). Seek Him with all your heart (Jeremiah 29:13). Trust Him even though you don't understand. Your relationship with Him is more priceless than all your worldly understanding. He is God, the One who laid the foundations of the earth! It's better to know Him than to know why.

Prayer

Lord, forgive me when I doubt Your wisdom and turn away from You because I don't understand. I know I can't possibly understand Your ways. The only thing that really matters is my relationship with You. No, Lord, I wasn't there when You laid the foundations of the earth. Help me give up the need to know why.

Thank You for all the blessings that come directly from Your loving and generous hands. Lord, everything good comes from You, and everything belongs to You. You are all I ever had. You are all I need. Lord, I want my life back. But I want You more.

A Future and a Hope

"For I know the plans I have for you," says the LORD.
"They are plans for good and not for disaster, to give you a
future and a hope. In those days when you pray, I will listen.
If you look for me wholeheartedly, you will find me."
JEREMIAH 29:11–13

For forty years Jeremiah served as God's faithful spokesperson to Judah. It was a high calling from God, except nobody listened. Once again, the nation had turned to idolatry and was headed for destruction. Jeremiah urged the people to turn from their sin and come back to God. He proclaimed God's truth and warned them what would happen if they didn't obey. But no one heeded his message. Instead, he was thrown into prison (Jeremiah 37); thrown into a cistern (Jeremiah 38); rejected by friends (Jeremiah 20:10), family (Jeremiah 12:6), and false prophets (Jeremiah 20:1–2). Of the last five kings he ministered under, all but King Josiah ignored his warnings and continued to lead the people astray (2 Kings 22–25). Jeremiah knew God's love for His people firsthand, and it grieved him to watch as they rejected His love and sealed their fate. Finally, it happened. His beloved country fell into the hands of the Babylonians in 586 BC (Jeremiah 39). No wonder they called him the "Weeping Prophet."

King Nebuchadnezzar took the elders, priests, prophets, and most of the people to Babylon and held them captive. But even after they had lost everything as a result of their rebellion, God continued to provide. Jeremiah wrote a letter from Jerusalem to the exiles in Babylon with God's instructions for how to survive their captivity and make the most of their circumstances: "Build homes and plan to stay. Plant gardens and eat the food you produce. Marry and have children. Then find spouses for them so that you may have many grandchildren. Multiply! Do not dwindle away! And work for the peace and prosperity of the city where I sent you into exile. Pray to the Lord for it, for its welfare will determine your welfare." He warned them not to listen to the prophets and fortune-tellers in the land of Babylon because He did not send them (Jeremiah 29:5–9).

And then He gave them a reason for hope—a promise to restore what was lost. They would live in Babylon for seventy years, but He would give them a new beginning where He would once again be in the center of their lives: " 'For I know the plans I have for you,' says the LORD. 'They are plans for good and not for disaster, to give you a future and a hope. In those days when you pray, I will listen. If you look for me wholeheartedly, you will find me' " (Jeremiah 29:10–13). Even in captivity, they could call on Him in confidence, He would hear their prayers and His presence would be with them. He promised to restore their fortunes and bring them home to their own land (Jeremiah 29:14). After King Cyrus of Persia conquered Babylon seventy years later, the Lord stirred his heart to allow the exiles to return to their homeland (Ezra 1), leading to a revival among the Jewish people and the rebuilding of the Temple.

Beloved, today it may seem like you have lost everything. You may be held captive by circumstances beyond your control or even mistakes of your own making. But rest assured you will not live in Babylon forever. Your God is a restoration expert. He can restore broken hearts, broken bodies, broken careers, broken relationships, and broken lives. For hundreds of years, He promised through the prophets to restore His fallen kingdom (Amos 9:11). He fulfilled the promise in Christ's resurrection

(Acts 15:16–17). Through the gift of redemption, He removed your sin and restored you to Himself (Colossians 1:20).

In the meantime, God will provide. Seek Him with all your heart and you *will* find Him. Pray and He will listen. His presence will be with you, His survival instructions will be clear and His grace will cover you. Move forward in obedience, making the most of your circumstances. He has not forgotten you because no situation can separate you from His love (Romans 8:38–39). You may not be certain what tomorrow may bring or when your breakthrough will come, but you can be certain of God. In Him, you have a future and a hope.

Prayer

Lord, forgive me for the times I've lost my way and turned my back on You like the Israelites. Thank You for meeting my every need, even when I've made mistakes! I seek You with all my heart, Lord. Thank You for hearing my prayers! Show me what to do next, Lord. Help me to be obedient in the midst of my unexpected circumstances.

Lord, I don't want to stay in Babylon forever! Please, restore me back to You. Release me from captivity and restore my fortunes! You alone know my future. You are good and You never change. Thank You that Your plans are good and full of hope!

Still Work to Do

There he came to a cave, where he spent the night.
But the LORD said to him, "What are you doing here, Elijah?"
1 KINGS 19:9

Linda was an assistant professor for a small East Coast university. She worked hard in a highly competitive environment to meet the teaching, research, and publication requirements for promotion. She thought she had the support of her department head and coworkers. Until she discovered she didn't. It was innocuous at first: whispered conversations that would stop abruptly when she walked into the room, not inviting her to lunch, or "forgetting" to include her on a meeting invite. Then it became more obvious. Her department head included blatant untruths in her performance evaluations and her coworkers collaborated on a list of unfounded grievances against her. She had no idea who she had offended or how. As a high performer and team player, her work was always stellar and inclusive. She had a string of successes the dean would consider for promotion. Yet her team was making an orchestrated effort to force her out. With each passing day, Linda grew more and more discouraged. When the toll on her physical and emotional health became more than she could bear, she quit.

———————

Now the prophet Elijah understood discouragement. Even after two huge spiritual victories against the powers of darkness, he, too, found himself emotionally drained, depressed, and abandoned. It all started when God sent him to tell King Ahab that He would be withholding rain for the next few years

(1 Kings 17:1). The northern kingdom of Israel had no faithful kings throughout its history, and King Ahab was no exception. He and his evil queen, Jezebel, brought the worship of the pagan god Baal into the kingdom, and God was not pleased.

Elijah hid for three years before God sent him back to the king. When they met, Elijah challenged Ahab and the people to make a choice between the one true God and Baal. So Ahab brought 850 pagan prophets for a showdown on Mount Carmel to test their power against the God of Elijah. When the Lord easily won the challenge, Elijah had all the prophets of Baal destroyed. Then he prayed and the Lord brought an end to the drought.

When Queen Jezebel heard what Elijah had done to her beloved prophets, she vowed to kill him. *Really, Lord?* It was more than he could bear, so he fled for his life. After traveling alone all day through the wilderness, he sat down under a solitary broom tree and prayed that he might die. "I have had enough, Lord," he said. "Take my life, for I am no better than my ancestors who have already died."

Totally defeated, he drifted off to sleep under the broom tree. *So tired.* Startled, he jolted awake. Someone was touching him. "Get up and eat!" a voice said. *An angel?* He looked around, and there beside his head was some bread baked on hot stones and a jar of water! So he ate and drank and lay down again to sleep.

Again, he felt someone touch him. *The angel.* "Get up and eat some more, or the journey ahead will be too much for you." So he got up again and ate and drank. *Strength, I need strength.* And then he set out on the journey. Somehow, he knew his destination was Mount Sinai, the mountain of God. The next forty days and nights all blurred together. The hot sun beat down as he stumbled up the rocky terrain. He struggled to breathe the thin air. He drifted in and out of consciousness. *So alone. So tired.* Finally, he arrived. *A cave. Must sleep.* And then a familiar voice: "What are you doing here, Elijah?" Elijah replied, "I have zealously served the LORD God Almighty. But the people of Israel have broken their covenant with You, torn down Your altars, and killed every one of Your prophets. I am the only one left and now they are trying to kill me, too."

The Lord continued to speak to him on the top of the mountain, not through a mighty windstorm, not through an earthquake, not through fire, but in the sound of a gentle whisper: "What are you doing here, Elijah?" And then He instructed him to go back the same way he came and anoint Hazael to be king of Aram, Jehu the grandson of Nimshi to be king of Israel, and Elisha son of Shaphat to replace him as prophet. Further, He promised to preserve the seven thousand others in Israel who had never bowed down to Baal. (Based on 1 Kings 18:16–45; 19:1–18.)

Even after succeeding in carrying out the Lord's plans, Elijah felt the darkness of his opposition pressing in around him. The discouragement overwhelmed him and rendered him unable to go on. He even forgot the others who had remained faithful to God through the nation's fall into wickedness. To lead him out of his depression, God first provided a time of solitude and rest. Then He confronted his emotions and pressed on him the need to complete his mission. The battle wasn't over and there was still work to do. In the same way, God provided Linda with an extended time to rest and seek Him when she reached emotional exhaustion and needed to escape. He reminded her of her past accomplishments, reaffirmed her calling, and eventually gave her a new assignment.

Beloved, if you are burdened and have reached a point of physical and emotional exhaustion in your work, come to Jesus and He will give you rest (Matthew 11:28). No matter what the enemy mounts up against you, no matter how the darkness closes in, God is on your side and nothing can steal your destiny (Romans 8:28, 31). His resources are unlimited, and His plans for your life are perfect (Ephesians 3:16; Psalm 18:30). He will give you everything you need to accomplish His purposes (Hebrews 13:21). Take time to rest. And then listen for His still small voice. Listen for your next assignment. There's still work to do.

Prayer

Lord, I have been faithful to You in my work and calling. But I'm so tired and discouraged. In spite of my successes, it seems like I'm always fighting back the opposition. I'm ready to run away, Lord. I'm ready to run into the wilderness to escape and be alone. And then I hear Your gentle whisper: "What are you doing here, beloved?"

Thank You for the plans and purposes You have for my life to advance Your Kingdom. Thank You for everything I have accomplished for Your glory. I do it all unto You, Lord! But I am so weary and my burdens are so heavy. Please give me Your sacred rest! Then show me what's next, Lord. I know there's still work to do!

Paradise Restored

And the LORD God made clothing from
animal skins for Adam and his wife.
GENESIS 3:21

He warned them not to eat from the tree in the middle of the garden. He said they must not even touch it or they would die. But the tree was so beautiful and its fruit looked so delicious! And what if the serpent was right? "You won't die!" he told her. "God knows that your eyes will be opened as soon as you eat it, and you will be like God, knowing both good and evil." She imagined being as wise as God and knowing everything He knew. The thought was tantalizing. Finally, she was convinced. Immediately after she had eaten the fruit and shared it with her husband, she knew it was a grave mistake. Something happened deep within her. It felt as though her innocence had been stolen along with the simplicity of her very existence. God's glory, His protective covering, was gone. She looked down and realized she and her husband were naked. Feeling vulnerable and ashamed, they rushed to gather some fig leaves to cover themselves.

And now they hid among the trees, waiting. God was walking about the garden like He always did when the cool evening breezes were blowing. She loved this time together when she and her husband would walk with Him. *Oh God, what have we done?* His voice interrupted her thoughts. "Where are you?" the Lord called out. Her husband replied, "I heard You walking in the garden, so I hid. I was afraid because I was naked." "Who told you that you were naked?" God asked. "Have you eaten from the tree whose fruit I commanded you not to eat?" He replied, "It was the woman You gave me who gave me the fruit, and I ate it." Then the Lord asked her, "What have you done?" "The serpent deceived me," she said. "That's why I ate it."

She could see the pain and heartbreak in His eyes. First, He had stern words for the serpent. He would grovel in the dust forever until the time came when he would be completely defeated. Then came the final verdict. He had no choice but to banish them from the garden. His perfect and holy nature allowed nothing less. If He allowed them to stay, they would be forever hiding from Him in a state of sin. Unlike the garden where everything was available, where they would live forever in His presence, her husband would now scratch a living from the ground and produce food by the sweat of his brow until they returned to the dust he came from. *Yes, they would surely die.* God made them clothing from animal skins and sent them on their way. And then He stationed mighty cherubim to the east of the Garden of Eden and a flaming sword to guard the way to the Tree of Life so they couldn't return. (Based on Genesis 3.)

It was always God's intention to live in intimacy with His children. He still longs to stroll with us as friends in the cool evening breeze. But Adam and Eve's grave mistake ushered sin into the paradise He created and broke off their relationship with Him. They were convinced they'd found a better way, but it was a way apart from His, a way that only led to destruction. And they were not alone. From that moment on, God's people repeatedly turned their hearts away from Him even though He promised to bless their obedience (Deuteronomy 28:11–12). For forty years He led a disobedient, defiant people through the wilderness, yet their clothes and sandals did not wear out and He provided for their every need (Deuteronomy 29:5–6). He extended this same mercy countless times, yet generations of people continued to go their own way.

But through it all, God had a perfect plan to restore the paradise Adam and Eve lost. He promised over three hundred times through the Old Testament prophets that He would send the anointed One who would rescue His people from their oppressors and establish a new Kingdom on earth. Finally, two thousand years ago, He sent His Son to recover what the enemy stole in the garden. By the time He came, the people were hopelessly oppressed by the Roman Empire. But He came to break the power of sin, to set things right again, and to initiate His Kingdom on earth (Matthew 12:28; Luke 4:18–20). His Kingdom is not just an eternal paradise we can hope to experience in the future, but a realm of power making *all* things possible today. In His Kingdom, by the power of His Spirit, there is intimacy, love, goodness, peace, joy, healing, and abundance, just as it was in the garden. His Kingdom is free from pain, suffering, hatred, and evil. There is nothing good lacking in the Kingdom of God.

Until Jesus comes back, there is still evil in the world. You will still have many trials on earth and, at times, you may feel like you are scratching the ground and barely earning a living. But you can take heart, because He has overcome the world (John 16:33)! Through His resurrection, He provided the full measure of grace to restore all things (Colossians 1:20). He will continue His work until it is finally finished on the day when He returns (Philippians 1:6). Until then, He is with you, just as He was with His children in the garden. As long as the earth remains, there will be planting and harvest, cold and heat, summer and winter, day and night (Genesis 8:22). Those who trust Him will lack no good thing (Psalm 34:10). Through His Son, He restored paradise forever.

Prayer

Once again, Lord, when I think of the Israelites and all the times they turned their backs on You, I am amazed by their stubbornness. And then I'm reminded, I am exactly the same! Forgive me, Lord, for all the times I want my own way instead of Yours and push You out of my life. Thank You for always extending Your mercy and providing for my every need, even in my disobedience.

Lord, You knew if You gave Your people free will, we would be like Adam and Eve and make poor choices. Thank You for having a plan to save me and for sending Your Son to pay the price for my disobedience and mistakes. You redeemed me from my sin and made me worthy to live in Your presence again. When You look at me You see a perfect child made righteous by the blood of Your Son (Romans 3:22; 5:9). Thank You, Lord, for taking back everything the enemy stole from me in the garden. Thank You for restoring paradise.

Jehovah-Jireh: Patty's Story

It was a crisp, beautiful morning, and she was feeling blessed. Not every January morning in Minnesota was this perfect. She marveled at the clear blue sky and the bright sun glistening off the snow. Her schedule was light, and she thought about what she would do to make the most of such a perfect day. It didn't last long. The light was green as she entered the intersection. She didn't see the car speeding toward her from the left until it was too late. It wouldn't have mattered anyway. There was nothing she could do.

Smack! She heard the sickening sound of crunching metal as the car crashed into her left front fender. The sheer impact sent her flying, her body slamming into the driver window. Before she could catch her breath, another *smack*! Her car crashed into a car to her right. Again, her body was thrown around the car as her right leg slammed into the front console. Her neck snapped back violently. Stunned, she quickly assessed the damage to her body. Thankfully, she was wearing her seat belt. Everything was a blur as the police arrived on the scene, followed by the tow truck. She knew before they told her. The car was totaled. Her perfect day was ruined by a young woman cruising through a red light at fifty miles per hour—talking on a cell phone.

The next few days were difficult. The true impact of her injuries began to manifest. Her body was racked with pain and from the bruising and torn muscles. On top of the physical challenges, she needed to replace her vehicle. She loved that car and she owned it free and clear. With her current budget constraints, she didn't know if she could afford a car payment. Even if she could, she was in so much physical pain she couldn't bear the thought of car shopping. She panicked. *God please! Help me.*

God answered her prayers. A kind neighbor happened to work as a salesman at the local Honda dealership. She called and asked him if he could keep his eye out for a suitable car. The very next day he drove home a 2008 Honda Civic that had just been traded in that morning. It was in wonderful condition and had every bell and whistle she could ever want. She loved it. *But how am I to pay for it?* God had that covered, too. With her totaled car settlement, along with a little savings of her own, she was able to purchase the car with an affordable payment. *Thank You, God.* He provided a *better* vehicle than the one she had lost.

But the real problems were just beginning. Sleeping, moving her limbs, standing up, sitting down, and basic living caused her excruciating pain. And she was unsure how to navigate the process of getting well. Pursuing the best treatment would be expensive, and her uncertainty about the out-of-pocket costs held her back. Again, she cried out to God, and He continued to bring the right people into her path. Trusted friends encouraged her to seek representation, and a coworker introduced her to his father, who just happened to be a seasoned personal injury attorney. Instead of referring her to a junior member of his law practice, he personally represented her. He advised her to take full advantage of whatever medical treatments would be necessary to restore her health because the insurance company would no longer be obligated to pay her accident-related medical expenses after six months. And she did. Physical therapy, chiropractic adjustments, cranial sacral massage, restorative massage, water therapy, and more filled her days. Through it all, Patty continued to stand in faith. She cried out to God, asking for justice and restoration for all the enemy had stolen from her—the additional car expense, attorney fees, time, missed work, rehabilitation, and all the pain and suffering. Then God led her to ask for something bold. She asked Him to make the enemy pay her back *seven* times what he had stolen. And she waited expectantly for her prayers to be answered.

God's counsel through this attorney proved wise. At the end of six months, she had no residual effects from a major car accident. Her pain was gone and her body was completely healed! Her attorney was amazed at her progress. He then said because there were no lingering symptoms, she would likely get an additional settlement on top of paying her medical bills. When they met six weeks later after everything had been settled, again her attorney was amazed. In all of his thirty years as a personal injury attorney, he had never seen a case settle like this one. Not only had the insurance company of the woman who hit her paid a premium to settle the case, but Patty's own insurance company also paid a premium. In addition, he had decided to take less than the amount they had agreed upon for his services. When he handed her the settlement check, she was stunned. The amount was exactly *seven* times more than her agent estimated when the accident first occurred. *Praise Jesus!*

Patty received her seven-fold payback. She was able to pay off all the debt and expenses resulting from the accident and then some. She gave all the glory to Jehovah-Jireh, the God who provides.

Ordinary People

*The members of the council were amazed when they saw the
boldness of Peter and John, for they could see that they were
ordinary men with no special training in the Scriptures.
They also recognized them as men who had been with Jesus.*

ACTS 4:13

For seven weeks, Peter and his small band of 120 followers
had been praying and waiting in Jerusalem for the Holy Spirit
to come. And He came, just as Jesus promised. Roaring like a
mighty windstorm, He filled the house where they were waiting
and settled on each of them like tongues of fire, with such power
that they all began speaking in other languages! Godly Jews
from many nations who were living in Jerusalem at the time
were beside themselves with wonder. But others accused them
of being drunk.

Emboldened by the Spirit, Peter found himself stepping
forward to speak. The words came without thinking and he
began preaching the Gospel with power in what would be
his first sermon as a great leader of the Church. He assured
the people that they were not drunk, but filled with the Spirit
of God as predicted long ago by the prophet Joel. Then he
said, "People of Israel, listen! God publicly endorsed Jesus
the Nazarene by doing powerful miracles, wonders, and signs
through Him, as you well know. But God knew what would
happen and His prearranged plan was carried out when Jesus
was betrayed. With the help of lawless Gentiles, you nailed
Him to a cross and killed Him."

He reminded them that God promised King David one of

his own descendents would sit on his throne and how David had prophesied the Messiah's resurrection. Then he said, "God raised Jesus from the dead, and we are all witnesses of this. Now He is exalted to the place of highest honor in heaven, at God's right hand. And the Father, as He had promised, gave Him the Holy Spirit to pour out upon us, just as you see and hear today. So let everyone in Israel know for certain that God has made this Jesus, whom you crucified, to be both Lord and Messiah!"

Peter's words pierced their hearts. When they asked him what they should do, he replied, "Each of you must repent of your sins and turn to God, and be baptized in the name of Jesus Christ for the forgiveness of your sins. Then you will receive the gift of the Holy Spirit." He continued preaching for a long time and three thousand people were baptized and added to the church that day. (Based on Acts 2:1–41.)

Peter continued to preach the Gospel with power, and the church continued to grow. After he performed the first miracle by healing a lame beggar by the Beautiful Gate (Acts 3:1–11), the religious leaders arrested him and John and brought them before the council to answer for their actions. Filled with the Holy Spirit, Peter responded boldly and concluded, " 'The stone that you builders rejected has now become the cornerstone.' There is salvation in no one else! God has given no other name under heaven by which we must be saved." The members of the council were amazed. They couldn't understand how ordinary men, with no special training in the scriptures could speak with such authority. They also recognized them as men who had been with Jesus (Acts 4:1–13).

It wasn't just Peter's lack of formal training that was so amazing. Peter had been a very unstable leader during Jesus' ministry, and he had some serious character flaws. He was known to be impulsive, brash, fearful, and to speak without thinking. In the middle of a violent storm, he jumped out of the boat and walked on water to meet Jesus, only to sink when he realized the reality of his circumstances (Matthew 14:22–33). He pulled Jesus aside and told Him *not* to go to Jerusalem where He was in danger of being killed, even though Jesus had already revealed His mission (Matthew 16:22–23). Still not understanding God's plan, he drew his sword and cut off a soldier's ear in the Garden of Gethsemane to protect Jesus when they came to arrest Him (John 18:10). He totally missed the point of servant leadership when Jesus washed his feet, and reacted by telling Him to wash the rest of him (John 13:6–9). He said he was ready to die for Jesus, but shortly after, he denied knowing Him three times (John 18:15–27). After Jesus was crucified and rose from the dead, Peter was so frustrated and discouraged, he simply went back to his old job of fishing (John 21:3).

Through it all, Peter had been with Jesus. It was Jesus who called him the rock upon which He would build His church, and all the powers of hell would not conquer it (Matthew 16:13–20). It was Jesus who forgave him, lifted him out of discouragement, and sent him out to feed His flock (John 18:15–19). It was Jesus who equipped him and empowered him to carry out his calling (Hebrews 13:21). Peter, an ordinary fisherman, would now fish for men (Matthew 4:19).

Jesus chose ordinary people like Peter whose lives could be changed by His love, in spite of their flaws. He invested in His relationships by spending time with His followers and teaching them the ways of the Kingdom. In the same way, He invests in you through His Spirit, His Word, worship, prayer, and gifted teachers. Just as God had a purpose for Peter, He has a purpose for you. He will give you exactly what you need at exactly the right time. He always equips and empowers those He calls (Hebrews 13:21). If God can use Peter, imagine how He might use you. You may be an ordinary person, but you've been with Jesus.

Prayer

Lord, I want to be Your trusted follower, I really do! But so often, I feel like I can't get it right! Sometimes, I don't understand what You want from me or what You're trying to teach me. Sometimes, I get so confused and discouraged I just go back to my old life. I go "fishing." Lord, through it all, thank You for grace and for not giving up on me!

I may be just an ordinary person, Lord, but in You, I am a masterpiece! You made me brand-new in Christ so I can do the good things You planned for me long ago (Ephesians 2:10). Thank You for Your promise to equip and empower me to do what You call me to do. I know You can use me to do extraordinary things because I've been with Jesus!

The Walls Came Down

It was by faith that the people of Israel marched around Jericho for seven days, and the walls came crashing down.
HEBREWS 11:30

Sarah had been working on the project for months, a major initiative that could ultimately impact millions of people. She had led countless hours of meetings to gather valuable information and worked through the appropriate channels to gain commitment and final approvals. The project team was excited about what they had accomplished, and they were ready to launch the next day. Because there were many moving parts, timing was of the essence. And then everything came to a screeching halt. Legal's senior attorney who had been on board all along suddenly had "grave concerns." A flurry of meetings took place. Tempers flared, and the situation escalated into a turf war among senior leaders from various departments. No solution could break down the walls of opposition that had come against her. Sarah was to lead another meeting first thing in the morning with all of them in attendance. They told her the project was doomed.

She went to bed that night with a knot in her stomach. She racked her brain for answers, but she kept running into the same wall. She thought of all the people who would be negatively impacted if the project failed, and the lost time and effort. *Please, God! Help me!* But no solutions came to mind, nothing that would satisfy a room full of concerned vice presidents, each vying for their own position. She drifted off to sleep and woke up early before sunrise. Before she could even think, there it was in her mind like it had been there all along. *The answer.* It made no logical sense. And it seemed way too easy. *God?* Yes.

All eyes were on Sarah when she opened the meeting that morning. Before the rancor could even begin, she shared her solution, a plan so simple it was almost ludicrous. And then she waited. *Silence.* Suddenly, the wall crumbled. Not one objection, not one question. The meeting that was scheduled for two hours ended in fifteen minutes. And the project launched on schedule.

Now Joshua ran into a wall. After Moses led the defiant Israelites through the desert for forty years, Joshua was the brave leader God chose to lead a new generation of people into the Promised Land. God had already led them on dry ground across the flood-level waters of the Jordan River (Joshua 3:14–17). Now, they faced the next daunting task. They had to get past the impenetrable wall surrounding Jericho, a city built thousands of years before he was even born. It wasn't just any wall. It was twenty-five feet high and twenty-five feet thick with soldiers standing on the top who could see for miles. The city was a symbol of power and strength, and the Canaanites believed it was invincible. *Lord, that's the city You want me to take?* Yes, the Lord said. "I have given you Jericho, its king, and all its strong warriors."

Joshua could see no way for them to win this battle on their own strength. But God had a plan, even if it made no human sense. "You and your fighting men should march around the town once a day for six days," God instructed. "Seven priests will walk ahead of the Ark, each carrying a ram's horn. On the seventh day you are to march around the town seven times, with the priests blowing the horns. When you hear the priests give one long blast on the rams' horns, have all the people shout as loud as they can. Then the walls of the town will collapse, and the people can charge straight into the town."

So Joshua called the people together and gave them the Lord's instructions. Seven priests with the rams' horns marched once around the town blowing their horns with the ark following behind. Some of the armed men marched in front of the priests and some behind the ark. Joshua warned, "Do not shout; do not even talk. Not a single word from any of you until I tell you to shout. Then shout!" For six days, they followed this pattern. On the seventh day, they marched around the town as they had done before, but this time they went around seven times. The seventh time, the priests sounded the long blast on their horns, and Joshua commanded, "Shout! For the LORD has given you the town!" When the people heard the sound of the rams' horns, they shouted as loud as they could. Sure enough, the walls of Jericho collapsed and the Israelites charged straight into the town and captured it. (Based on Joshua 6:1–20.)

God gave him the city and the plan to conquer it, but Joshua had to execute the plan, even though it seemed ludicrous and he didn't understand it. Unlike the generation before them, the people faithfully and patiently obeyed God without complaining or questioning His guidance. God made it clear the victory was dependent on Him and not their weapons or experience. He had already won the battle and they were fighting from a place of victory. As they marched in procession, the ark was symbolic of His presence (Exodus 25:22) and the trumpets were a reminder that the victory came from God (Numbers 10:9).

Today, the enemy may be erecting walls like Sarah encountered—walls that cause trouble or block His purposes in your life. But you also fight against a *defeated* enemy. You are more than a conqueror in Christ (Romans 8:35–37). No wall is too tall or too thick when God is on your side (Romans 8:31). Bring Him into the center of your battle. Listen for His strategy and act in faith, even when His plan makes no worldly sense. Watch those walls come crashing down!

Prayer

Lord, there is a tall, thick wall in front of me today and I know I can't break through it on my own power. I can do nothing apart from You (John 15:15). Thank You that I fight from a place of victory. Help me, Lord! I wait in Your presence. Show me what to do!

Lord, Your thoughts are higher than mine and Your ways are far beyond my imagination (Isaiah 55:8). Please give me the courage and the boldness to act in faith, even when Your plans make no sense. I know obedience to You requires my trust, not my understanding. Lord, thank You for always being on my side. In You, no wall can block my destiny. Lord, I march! I shout! And I watch my walls come crashing down!

Rebuild the Wall!

*Then I told them about how the gracious hand of God had been on me,
and about my conversation with the king. They replied at once,
"Yes, let's rebuild the wall!" So they began the good work.*
NEHEMIAH 2:18

It was always his mother's dream that he would escape the
poverty, crowds, pollution, and limited opportunities in India.
Her dream was realized when Jahesh and his wife, Prisha, found
good jobs in the United States. He was a corporate accountant
and she worked in banking. They owned a nice home, had two
children, and lived a typical middle-class, first-world life; until
God had a different idea. He intensified the burden on their
hearts for the hopelessness in their homeland, especially among
the untouchable class. They prayed for clarity and direction.
And God said, "Go." So they left their comfortable lives behind
and moved back to India to build into the lives of thousands
of broken and impoverished people. Through their nonprofit
ministry, they plant churches; disciple pastors and members;
and provide financial support, schools, and biblically based
training to help them create sustainable lives and communities.
In spite of opposing forces intent on destroying the Christian
faith, God continues to protect and multiply their ministry.

It was a Memorial Day weekend in central Texas, the
beginning of the tourist season that so many depended on
for their livelihood. No one expected over thirteen inches of
rain to fall on saturated ground in just a few hours' time or
the record-setting flash flood that roared through the town. A

wall of water peaking at forty-five feet claimed fourteen lives, destroyed twenty-one hundred homes and area businesses, and washed out roads, bridges, and most of the town's infrastructure. One couple lost both their home and their resort business, a mainstay in the community that had been in the family for generations. The cost of rebuilding both would far exceed their life savings and any government assistance or insurance proceeds, not to mention the lost income. But they prayed and believed God was calling them to stay and rebuild their home and business. They trusted He would provide, and He did. A local government group assisted by donations, and volunteers, stepped in to lead the rebuilding efforts. And from a thousand miles away, a church group came many times to help with cleanup and rebuilding until the damaged cabins were restored.

God has always worked through people to rebuild, restore, and accomplish the impossible, and He often shapes our personalities, strengths, and training to prepare us for His purposes. Nehemiah faced an impossible task, but God knew He had the character, perseverance, and leadership skills to succeed. He held a comfortable position working for the Persian King Artaxerxes when he learned that the people in his homeland, Jerusalem, were in great trouble and disgrace. Seventy years earlier, the exiles returned and rebuilt the Temple, but the wall of the great city remained in shambles and the gates destroyed by fire. The people were disorganized and discouraged and the city defenseless.

Upon learning this news, Nehemiah sat down and wept. For days, he fasted and prayed and repented on behalf of his family and nation. At the end of his heartfelt prayer time, he knew what he had to do. God was calling him to leave the comforts and wealth of Persia. God was calling him home. With the king's blessing and assistance along the way, he departed for the long journey. But upon his arrival, he was met with opposition. There were many who had settled in the area during the years of Jewish captivity who hated the Jews and didn't want their city to be rebuilt. But Nehemiah was undeterred. He went around the town for several days, inspecting the broken walls and developing a strategy before making his case to the religious and political leaders in the city. They gave their blessing to rebuild the wall, but still his opponents antagonized him. Unmoved, Nehemiah said, "The God of heaven will help us succeed. You have no stake or claim in Jerusalem."

Nehemiah executed his plan. Under his leadership, all the citizens did their part to rebuild the section of the wall closest to them, while his opponents continued to mock them. Finally, when the wall was half built, his enemies made plans to fight him and the workers grew tired and fearful and began to complain. Again, Nehemiah went to the Lord for strength. He encouraged the workers. And from then on, only half the men worked while the other half stood guard with spears, shields, bows, and coats of armor. The laborers carried their load with one hand and held a weapon with the other, and all of them had a sword belted to their side. Trusting God to fight for them, they worked from sunrise to sunset for fifty-two days until the wall was complete. (Based on Nehemiah 1–6.)

Nehemiah's model was to pray and take action. He saw the problem, shared his concerns with God, acknowledged God's power to help, listened for direction, and then took steps to fix it. He organized, supervised, encouraged, confronted opposition, and kept going until he finished, all while praying for God's work to succeed. Has God given you a vision to rebuild something the enemy has destroyed? Has he laid a burden on your heart to restore broken homes, broken lives, or broken communities? Then pray like Nehemiah. With God's power and direction, you, too, can accomplish the impossible, because you work for Him. He will give you everything you need to succeed: wisdom, resources, protection from your enemies, and strength to carry out His plan. He will never let you fail. Beloved, when His gracious favor is upon you, it's time to rebuild the wall.

Prayer

I praise You, Lord! I thank You for all You have done in my life. Please forgive my indifference toward the desperate needs of others. Please put a burden on my heart for the things that break Yours. Hear my sorrows, Lord, and give me Your vision for the brokenness right in front of me. Lord, give me clarity and show me what to do. When You call me forward to rebuild and restore, please give me the courage to step out in faith, even if it means leaving the comforts of my current life.

Protect me, Lord! I know when I step forward to advance Your Kingdom, the enemy doesn't like it (1 John 3:13)! Help me persevere in the face of opposition. I need Your strength, Lord. In You, I can accomplish anything You call me to do. Thank You for pouring Your gracious favor upon me! Help me endure until the end.

Road to Damascus

As he was approaching Damascus on this mission, a light from heaven suddenly shone down around him. He fell to the ground and heard a voice saying to him, "Saul! Saul! Why are you persecuting me?"

ACTS 9:3–4

Saul was a brilliant scholar and an esteemed Pharisee. He had received the finest training in Jewish law and tradition and sincerely believed the Christian movement was a danger to Judaism. So he made it his personal mission to hunt down and destroy every follower of Jesus. He was even present at the martyr Stephen's murder, giving approval and holding the clothes of those who stoned him to death for teaching about Jesus (Acts 22:20). Like his colleagues at the time, his intellect and social standing blinded him to some three hundred prophesies that spoke of the coming of the Messiah. The Creator of the universe came down to earth, exactly as Saul's beloved scriptures described, and Saul missed it. And then everything changed on the road to Damascus.

Saul was traveling there with permission from the high priest to arrest Christians and bring them back to Jerusalem in chains. Suddenly, a brilliant light from heaven beamed down on him. Completely overwhelmed, he fell to the ground and covered his eyes, not understanding what was happening. And then he heard a voice saying, "Saul! Saul! Why are you persecuting Me?" *God? Is it You? How am I persecuting You?* "Who are You, Lord?" Saul asked. And the voice replied, "I am Jesus, the one you are persecuting! Now get up and go into the city, and you will be told what you must do." Stunned, he struggled to his feet. The light had forced his eyes closed, but when he opened them, he was blind. The men with him stood speechless. They heard the sound of someone's voice but saw no one. "My eyes!" he cried. So they led him by the hand to Damascus. When they delivered him to the house where he was staying, he did not eat or drink. He sat in silence and prayed. *Jesus, is it You I have been persecuting? Is it really You, Messiah?* His heart ached as God began to speak to him in visions.

Three days later, the Lord spoke to a believer in Damascus named Ananias in a vision. "Go over to Straight Street, to the house of Judas," He said. "When you get there, ask for a man from Tarsus named Saul. He is praying to Me right now. I have shown him a vision of a man named Ananias coming in and laying hands on him so he can see again." Stunned, Ananias objected. "I've heard about the terrible things this man has done to the believers in Jerusalem! And he is authorized by the leading priests to arrest everyone who calls upon Your name." But the Lord said, "Go, for Saul is My chosen instrument to take My message to the Gentiles and to kings, as well as to the people of Israel."

So Ananias went and found Saul and laid his hands on him and prayed. Instantly the scales fell from Saul's eyes, and he regained his sight. Saul was baptized and later began preaching in the synagogues saying, "Jesus is indeed the Son of God!" And all who heard him were amazed. (Based on Acts 9:1–21.)

God had to heal Saul's spiritual blindness in order to shift his fierce passion from persecuting Christians to preaching about Christ. It's no surprise his Pharisee friends wanted to kill him for his defection and the followers of Jesus had to be convinced to accept him (Acts 9:23, 26–28). After spending three years in the desert region of Arabia to be alone with God (Galatians

1:17–24), he became known as Paul, the apostle to the Gentiles. He preached the Gospel with power, and his ministry stretched throughout the Roman Empire and into the hearts of every believer through his New Testament letters to the early church.

Paul and his Pharisee friends let their superior intellect and social standing keep them blind to the Messiah when He was right under their noses. The same was true of Joe, a successful modern-day physician. He didn't persecute Christians, but like Paul, he spent years trying to convince himself and others that Jesus wasn't God's Son who died for the sins of the world. As a science-minded intellectual, Dr. Joe needed proof. God didn't confront him on the road to Damascus, but He didn't stop pursuing him. Over the years, He gently revealed Himself until Dr. Joe was convinced. He received Jesus as Lord and was baptized at the age of eighty-six, five weeks before he passed away.

Sometimes we can be blind to what God is doing when we think we are strong and wise and doing His will. We can even miss great movements of God because we are stuck in "old wineskins" and our limited human understanding of God and His ways (Mark 2:22). All the good things we are doing for God can become ritualistic or even oppose His heart and His Kingdom plans. For example, we can be legalistic and judge people caught in sin instead of loving them into the Kingdom. Or we can play it safe and not reach out to pray for people in need, when God wants us to be spiritually bold so He can show His power. These are the times He may lovingly highlight our spiritual blindness and open our eyes to get us on track.

Paul's story gives us great hope. God will use you for His glory, no matter what you have believed or what you have done. He has great plans and purposes for your life, and He will never stop pursuing you. He won't let you stay blind forever. You might even meet Him on the road to Damascus.

Prayer

Lord, show me where I am blind to Your plans and purposes for my life, my family, my church, and my nation. Forgive me when I've been so caught up in routines, rituals, and habits that I have not perceived the brand-new things You are doing right under my nose (Isaiah 43:19). I'm sorry for the times I have unknowingly persecuted You out of ignorance or blindness to Your heart for the needs of others around me.

Thank You for the plans and purposes You have for my life. Thank You that You never stop pursuing me when I think I am strong and wise and doing Your will! I don't want to be stuck anymore! Open my eyes, Lord. I want to see!

Do the Work

Then David continued, "Be strong and courageous, and do the work.
Don't be afraid or discouraged, for the LORD God, my God, is with you.
He will not fail you or forsake you. He will see to it that all the
work related to the Temple of the LORD is finished correctly.
1 CHRONICLES 28:20

For thirty-three years of his forty-year reign, King David ruled from Jerusalem and enjoyed a long life of wealth and honor. Although he made mistakes, he loved the Lord and learned to give His whole heart to God. Toward the end of his reign, David summoned all the officials of Israel to Jerusalem to share God's plan for Israel and His promise to David's descendents. He told them of his dream to build a Temple to replace the Tabernacle, where the Ark of the Covenant could rest permanently. But God had denied his request. He made all the necessary preparations for building it, but God said, "You must not build a Temple to honor My name, for you are a warrior and have shed much blood."

Then he told them that God chose his son Solomon to succeed him on the throne of Israel and to build the Temple of the Lord. In front of God and all the leaders of Israel, he gave this charge to his son: "Be careful to obey all the commands of the LORD your God, so that you may continue to possess this good land and leave it to your children as a permanent inheritance. Learn to know the God of your ancestors intimately. Worship and serve Him with your whole heart and a willing mind. For the LORD sees every heart and knows every plan and thought. If you seek Him, you will find Him. So take this seriously. The LORD has chosen you to build a Temple as His sanctuary."

David gave Solomon the plans for the Temple and its surroundings, including every room, the courtyards, and the treasuries. He gave instructions concerning the work of the various priests and Levites in the Temple and specifications for the items that were to be used for worship. He instructed Solomon how much gold and silver should be used to make the items needed for service, including the lamp stands, lamps, tables, meat hooks, basins, pitchers, dishes, the altar of incense, and the gold cherubim whose wings were stretched out over the Ark of the Lord's Covenant. And then he told his son, "Every part of this plan was given to me in writing from the hand of the Lord."

Then David encouraged Solomon. "Be strong and courageous, and do the work. Don't be afraid or discouraged, for the Lord God, my God, is with you. He will not fail you or forsake you. He will see to it that all the work related to the Temple of the Lord is finished correctly. The various divisions of priests and Levites will serve in the Temple of God. Others with skills of every kind will volunteer, and the officials and the entire nation are at your command."

Finally, King David turned to the entire assembly and said, "My son Solomon, whom God has clearly chosen as the next king of Israel, is still young and inexperienced. The work ahead of him is enormous, for the Temple he will build is not for mere mortals—it is for the Lord God Himself!" (Based on 1 Chronicles 28–29:1.)

———————————————

Enormous was an understatement. Just imagine how the young and inexperienced Solomon felt at that very moment. He's not only faced with the challenge of stepping into his famous father's shoes as king of all Israel, but with the daunting task of building an earthly home for the Creator of the universe. There were no engineers, no bulldozers, no backhoes, no cranes, no trucks, no explosives, no power, and no fuel in 970 BC. All he had were verbal instructions, stacks of raw material, and a plethora of volunteer workers, skilled stonemasons, carpenters, and craftsmen, all awaiting his orders.

How much raw material? The amount was staggering. David had gathered innumerable cedar logs, stone for the walls, nearly 4,000 tons of gold, 40,000 tons of silver, and so much iron and bronze that it could not be weighed, as well as great quantities of onyx, other precious stones, costly jewels, and all kinds of fine stone and marble. In addition, the king personally donated more than 112 tons of gold and 262 tons of refined silver from his own treasuries, and the other leaders of Israel gave about 188 tons of gold, 10,000 gold coins, 375 tons of silver, 675 tons of bronze, and 3,750 tons of iron (1 Chronicles 22:2–4, 14–16; 29:2–7). Yes, enormous was an understatement. Yet, with God's power, Solomon finished the Temple of the Lord and his own royal palace and completed everything he had planned to do (2 Chronicles 7:11). It took him twenty years, 70,000 common laborers, 80,000 men to quarry stone, and 3,600 foremen to supervise the work (1 Kings 9:10; 2 Chronicles 2:2).

Does the work in front of you today feel enormous? Insurmountable? Overwhelming? Sometimes the sheer magnitude of a job, the risks involved, and the pressure to succeed can cause paralyzing fear. We can become so afraid and so discouraged, we don't know where to begin. But David's counsel to Solomon applies to us today. And he made it clear what is needed for success. Seek God and you will find Him. Worship and serve Him with your whole heart and a willing mind. He will give you everything you need and see to it that all the work is finished correctly. He is with you, and He will not fail or forsake you. Be strong and courageous and do the work!

Prayer

Yes, Lord, there are times when the work in front of me feels overwhelming! I can't see where to begin, and when I do, I'm afraid of failing or never finishing. Lord, in whatever I do, help me to work at it with all my heart, as if working for You rather than for people! I know that I will receive an inheritance from the Lord as a reward, because it is You alone that I am serving (Colossians 3:23–24).

Help me get started, Lord! Help me bring this work to completion. I give You all my worries and fear. In exchange, thank You for giving me everything I need and for making sure all the work is finished correctly. You are with me and You will not fail or forsake me. Give me courage, Lord. Help me be strong. Help me to do the work!

Jevovah-Jireh: Suzanne's Story

Cancer changed everything. Suzanne had owned a successful consulting practice before the diagnosis. She even went to church every Sunday. But then she met Jesus. His promises became more than words on a page, and He became more than a distant God who died so she could go to heaven someday. He healed her from cancer and restored her completely. She marvels at how He used that year of intense treatment and uncertainty to radically change her life. Her life had taken a course correction, and she was certain she understood what God was doing. He was being true to His promise in Romans 8:28 to cause "everything to work together for the good of those who love God and are called according to his purpose." She started a ministry to help others battling cancer and, God willing, she would use her professional skills as a communication consultant to write encouraging books that would help others facing similar life trials. And her flexible work schedule would make it all possible.

God's hand of favor was upon her for the first two books. She worked hard and doors miraculously opened with a well-known Christian publisher, confirming her newfound purpose and calling. Then she hit a wall. The publisher turned down her next six proposals. Sales were not what they had expected or hoped. As an author without an agent, she tried unsuccessfully to publish with so many different publishers she lost count. For three years she tried to find an agent who would represent her and finally gave up. *What are You doing, God?* Eventually, she concluded that two books on the market were all God planned, books that she could directly use in her ministry to bless others.

During the same years she was struggling with her writing career, she was pouring herself into her large church, both into leadership and ministry. She spent countless volunteer hours leading as a church elder, serving, teaching classes, praying for and caring for sick and hurting people. As her time and attention gradually shifted away from her consulting business, her income slowly dried up. But it didn't matter. *God must have a different plan.* Obediently, she focused her time on her calling, until her church eventually commissioned her as a pastor. Through prophetic words, encouragement from those she served with, and her own encounters with God, she became convinced that part of that plan was full-time employment at the church where she had obediently served so closely with senior leaders and decision makers. Through it all, she trusted God and His timing for her life and ministry.

Eventually, she found herself working full-time without the benefit of making a living. Her husband's income covered their expenses. But depending on him exclusively for their livelihood while she continued to write on speculation and volunteer at church made her feel guilty. She wasn't contributing. She wrestled with God. She knew He was refining her, and she knew she needed to trust Him to provide. She thought surely this would all work out when her church hired her in a full-time staff pastoral role.

Only they didn't. Four times in three years they had the opportunity to do so and each time they hired someone else. And each time, she felt more misunderstood, more rejected, more hurt, and more betrayed by the leaders in her church whom she had faithfully served alongside for years. Most of all, she felt trapped. She saw no way of escaping her volunteer leadership roles and the teams she loved and had invested in. Yet, she couldn't walk in the fullness of her calling in the church she dearly loved, the church that she had so faithfully served, where she cared for a flock who viewed her as one of their pastors. *What are You doing, God?* When she finally realized she was in full burnout mode, she sought counseling. She doubted her calling, but worse than that, she doubted whether she really heard God. She wondered if it was time to leave the ministry and go back to the marketplace where she could escape the pain of deep betrayal and earn a real living.

While all this was happening, Suzanne's husband was also in a job crisis. His current position was a poor fit for his passions and skills, fraught with leadership dysfunction, and he was tasked with impossible, unrealistic goals. No matter how hard he worked, the results didn't come. He sunk into a deep depression. Her decision was made. Since employment at her church was not an option, she must leave her calling of vocational ministry behind, go back into the marketplace, and work so he could quit. It was her time to carry the weight, and his time to rest and heal.

But again, God had a different plan. A year earlier, she signed with a literary agent in what she now realizes was a miraculous move of God. She didn't find this agent. He found her. About the time she was ready to launch into fulltime job-search mode, she received an unexpected call on her birthday. Her agent landed her a two-book contract from a major publisher. *Really, God? Now?* She and her husband prayed and agreed she had no choice but to write the books. Since writing is usually fulltime work with a nominal income, this would mean no job with benefits for her and the long-term responsibility for their livelihood continuing to rest on her husband's shoulders.

During the year she wrote the two books, they trusted in God's provision. Her husband transitioned out of his toxic work environment and had an amazing season of healing and restoration. As she struggled to forgive those in the church, God continued to heal her by revealing the motives of her own heart, ministering to her directly through her own writing, and confirming that He alone is the perfect spiritual father and provider. Breakthrough came when she and her husband had the opportunity to travel to Israel together. In the Garden of Gethsemane, God profoundly showed her that the sins of those who wounded her so deeply were in the cup Jesus drank, right along with hers.

Today, while she stores up treasures in heaven, her husband is employed at a job he loves. She writes full-time and teaches and ministers as a volunteer pastor, with prayerful boundaries, in the same large church. She still wonders whether God was preparing her for vocational ministry in the church where she grew to know Him, love Him, and serve Him. But she also believes He doesn't trump the free will of man. And she knows the enemy wants nothing more than to steal her destiny. She firmly believes forgiveness is the path to healing and freedom, and has had many opportunities to walk it out publicly. As she continues to choose forgiveness over bitterness, God continues to give her the power and grace to love and honor the leaders in her church. She knows He always redeems, regardless of her own mistakes or the mistakes of others. Even if others might miss her destiny and purpose, God never does. Jehovah-Jireh *always* provides. He always provides a way. And He continues to make all things work for good according to His purposes for those who love Him.

Wait for It

*This vision is for a future time. It describes the end,
and it will be fulfilled. If it seems slow in coming, wait patiently,
for it will surely take place. It will not be delayed.*
HABAKKUK 2:3

Cassie has been waiting for God to provide a husband to love and cherish her, and to share her life with since her parents sent her off to college. One by one, her friends have married and started families. But Cassie is in her mid-thirties and still waiting. It's not like she hasn't had opportunities. She's had many. But the chemistry isn't right. And when the chemistry is "spot on," and the spark ignites, something from the past always seems to keep the relationship from moving forward and douses the flame. She finds herself in a repeating cycle of dating men with very promising destinies who are broken and unavailable. And after her most recent heartbreak, she is convinced that hope deferred indeed does make the heart sick (Proverbs 13:12). In fact, the delay of an eagerly awaited, unfilled longing can feel the same as suffering from a lingering physical disease. *What are You doing in this, God? How long must I wait?*

The prophet Habakkuk wondered, too. He lived at a time in Judah when evil and injustice had the upper hand, and he cried out to God, "How long must I call for help?" (Habakkuk 1:2–3). In the midst of the injustice and evil all around him, God told the prophet he must wait for His plans and purposes to come to pass. In her time of endless waiting, Cassie can't help but wonder: God, does a delay mean the answer is no? Does it mean

You don't love me? Are You punishing me for something? Is there something wrong with me? How long must I call for help? To all her questions, God's answer is simple. Wait for it. It will be fulfilled. If it seems slow in coming, wait patiently, for it will surely take place. It will not be delayed. God's goodness and His provision are not determined by her current circumstances. He is a faithful Father who passionately loves her, regardless of her own faithfulness or past mistakes (2 Timothy 2:19; Romans 3:3; 8:38–39). God's answer is *wait for it*.

Maybe you find yourself in a place of waiting, just like Cassie. Waiting patiently has always been challenging, especially today. We live in an instant world, and we are used to instant results. Mr. Google can answer almost any question in seconds. Why write and send a note or letter by snail mail when we can send an e-mail or simply text? We can make dinner in five minutes with salad-in-a-bag and a microwave oven. Social media makes it possible to share photos with friends and family in a matter of seconds. With instant movies, instant news, instant replay, instant coffee, instant *everything*, waiting has become a lost art.

We really have two choices when we are waiting for God's provision. We can pray a few times and then give up when things don't come instantly or on our timetable. We can become discouraged or even angry at God for not understanding our circumstances and meeting the desperate longings of our heart. Or we can wait expectantly, remain hopeful, and believe that any minute our breakthrough will come. The very essence of faith is waiting in confidence for the things we hope for and to be certain of things yet unseen (Hebrews 11:1). In times of waiting, the seeds of our faith take root as we cling to God and His promises. As we trust in Him, He makes His home in our hearts, and our roots of faith grow deep into His love that keeps us strong (Ephesians 3:17; Colossians 2:7). We can be confident and expectant of a bountiful harvest when the seeds of faith fall on good soil and are allowed to grow (Matthew 13:23).

Waiting on God is not new to a life of faith. Abraham and Sarah waited twenty-five years for the birth of their promised son Isaac (Genesis 21:2). After the prophet Samuel anointed David as king of Israel, he waited fifteen years before becoming king of Judah and more than twenty years before he reigned over all of Israel (2 Samuel 2:1–5:5). Joseph spent thirteen years in slavery and prison before he became ruler of Egypt (Genesis 37–41). It was seven hundred years after Isaiah prophesied the coming Messiah, before Jesus came to redeem a broken world (Isaiah 7:14). And today, we are still waiting for Jesus to return and bring all things to completion (Matthew 25:36–37).

Waiting for something we don't yet have is painful and difficult. Yet, God wants us to wait patiently and confidently (Romans 8:25). He will never abandon you in your time of waiting (Hebrews 13:5). As you trust in Him, He will give you new strength and show you His love and compassion like never before (Isaiah 40:31; 30:18). Always remember the Lord's faithfulness to you in the past. Ponder His work and meditate on His mighty deeds, giving thanks with a whole heart for what He has done (Psalm 77:12; 9:1). In confident hope, be patient and keep on praying (Romans 12:12). If your provision seems slow in coming, wait patiently, for it will surely take place. It will not be delayed. And when it does, a longing fulfilled is a tree of life—sweet, satisfactory, and reviving to the soul (Proverbs 13:12). Wait for it and it *will* be fulfilled.

Prayer

Lord, You know exactly what I'm waiting for right now, and the delay is surely making my heart sick! Jehovah-Jireh, how long must I wait for Your provision? Yet, I thank You, Lord, that Your faithfulness does not depend on mine, and Your love for me is unconditional. You are always a good God and Your delays are not denials.

Lord, forgive me for my impatience. I'm sorry for being angry and discouraged when You have not moved according to my timetable. Help me to wait expectantly for my breakthrough to come. While I wait in Your presence, may my roots of faith grow deep in the soil of Your love. I ponder Your mighty deeds, Lord, and I thank You for Your faithfulness. You know the longing of my heart. Help me to wait for it.

Eyes to See

And Elisha prayed, "Open his eyes, LORD, so that he may see."
Then the LORD opened the servant's eyes, and he looked and saw
the hills full of horses and chariots of fire all around Elisha.
2 KINGS 6:17 NIV

Panicked, John poured his heart out to the prayer minister at his church. He had been promoted into a new position a few months ago and the job has been tough. Some of his coworkers complained about his performance, and their concerns had escalated to human resources and his boss. The complaints have left him shaken and heavyhearted. He is embarrassed and he feels incompetent. More importantly, he feels as though his coworkers don't believe he is qualified for the job. "I can't afford to lose this job," he cried out in desperation. "I am the main source of income for my family! I can't shake this fear, I can't stop worrying, and I can't sleep at night. Please pray!" As the prayer minister prayed for protection and favor with his boss and coworkers, God laid the following words on her heart: "Don't be afraid. For there are more on our side than on theirs!"

These powerful words were originally spoken by the prophet Elisha. When the king of Aram was at war with Israel, he grew frustrated to learn that it was Elisha, not a traitor in his own ranks, who was keeping the King of Israel informed of his battle plans. Upon locating Elisha in Dothan, the enraged and determined king sent horses, chariots, and a strong force of his men by night to capture him there. Early the next morning, Elisha's servant went out and panicked when he discovered an army of horses and chariots surrounding the city. "Oh no, my lord! What shall we do?" he cried out to Elisha. But the prophet calmly answered, "Don't be afraid. Those who are with us are more than those who are with them." And then, he prayed, "Open his eyes, Lord, so that he may see."

The Lord answered Elisha's prayer. This time when the servant looked, he saw the hills full of horses and chariots of fire all around Elisha. As the enemy came down toward him, Elisha prayed again. "Strike this army with blindness." Again, the Lord answered and struck the army with blindness. Then Elisha told them, "This is not the road and this is not the city. Follow me, and I will lead you to the man you are looking for." And he led them right into Samaria, Israel's capital city. Elisha asked the Lord to open their eyes, and when He did, Aram's men realized they were as good as dead. But instead of killing the captives, Elisha advised the King of Israel to prepare a feast for them and send them back home. From that point on, the king of Aram stopped raiding Israel's territory. (Based on 2 Kings 6:1–23.)

Elisha's servant was no longer afraid when the Lord opened his eyes and he saw heaven's mighty army at his defense. In John's battle, the problem wasn't with God's power, but his own eyesight. God was doing much more than he could see through his human eyes alone. God was calling him to see his insurmountable problem through eyes of faith, and allow the truth of heaven's infinite resources to quell his fears. John discovered that God's army is much greater in number than those who mounted up an attack against him. God was on his side (Romans 8:31). He kept his job, facts were separated from lies, and the conflicts were resolved as he showed mercy to his attackers and trusted God for the outcome.

When you face difficulties like John faced, you can trust God's spiritual resources are there, even when you cannot see. An entire supernatural realm of power exists beyond the natural. The Lord's angels are there, spiritual beings He created to care for the hurting and protect the helpless (Hebrews 1:14). God sent an angel to shut the mouth of lions (Daniel 6:22). He sent an angel to rescue Peter from prison and certain death (Acts 12:7–10). He sent an angel to strengthen Elijah when he was depressed and ready to give up (1 Kings 19:5–7). He promises to order His angels to protect you wherever you go, to hold you up with their hands so you won't even hurt your foot on a stone (Psalm 91:11–12). His angels literally camp around you and deliver you from trouble (Psalm 34:7)!

When a crisis comes and fear threatens to paralyze you, will you see through the eyes of the world or the eyes of faith? Don't be tempted to think like everyone else thinks or believe that some plan conceived behind closed doors will be the end of you. If you trust in God alone, you don't need to panic or fear anything else. He will keep you safe (Isaiah 8:11–14). Just because you can't see with human eyes doesn't mean He isn't working on your behalf. You have all of heaven's armies at your disposal. Can you see it? The hills surrounding you are filled with horses and chariots of fire! Ask the Lord for eyes to see.

Prayer

Lord, when I'm afraid, I know the problem isn't Your lack of power—it is my eyesight! Forgive me when I limit Your power to what I can see, hear, and feel around me. I know You and all of heaven's resources are working on my behalf, even when I cannot see. Thank You for Your angels that are camped around me, protecting me wherever I go and rescuing me when I'm in deep trouble.

Yes, Lord, I need spiritual glasses! Help me see through the eyes of faith! Please let the truth of Your power and presence penetrate deep into my spirit. Let the truth of Your mighty heavenly resources dispel all my fears! I want to see like Elisha's servant! Lord, give me eyes to see!

Obedience Is Better

But Samuel replied, "What is more pleasing to the Lord: your burnt offerings and sacrifices or your obedience to his voice? Listen! Obedience is better than sacrifice, and submission is better than offering the fat of rams."
1 Samuel 15:22

Saul had great potential. As the first God-appointed king of Israel, he was tall, handsome, courageous, a skillful soldier, and a man of action. Everything started out great for him in his forty-two-year reign. God provided all the authority and resources he needed to be an effective leader. He successfully led the people into several battles against Israel's enemies, including a stunning victory against the Ammonites. But he was also impulsive, impatient, and tended to overstep his bounds. Saul wanted to do things *his* way. And that became his downfall.

After his son Jonathan attacked and destroyed the Philistine outpost at Geba and the news quickly spread among the Philistines, Saul knew big trouble was coming. He summoned the entire Israelite army to join him at Gilgal to face a mighty Philistine army of three thousand chariots, six thousand charioteers, and as many warriors as the grains of sand on the seashore! Saul's men saw they were hard pressed by the enemy so they ran and hid in caves, thickets, rocks, holes, and cisterns. Some of them crossed the Jordan River and escaped into the land of Gad and Gilead.

Meanwhile, Saul stayed at Gilgal; his men were trembling with fear, while he grew more and more frantic. Earlier, the Lord's prophet Samuel had given him instructions for this very moment: "Go down to Gilgal ahead of me. I will join you there to sacrifice burnt offerings and peace offerings. You must wait for seven days until I arrive and give you further instructions." Saul waited. One day, two, then three, each day passing while he watched his troops rapidly slip away. And still no Samuel. *Where is he? Doesn't he know the danger we're in? We could lose everything!* But Samuel still didn't come. Finally, on the seventh day, Saul snapped. "Bring me the burnt offering and the peace offerings!" he demanded. He couldn't help himself. He had to take charge. God's law required a sacrifice. It didn't really matter how the sacrifice was made, as long as it was made, he reasoned. So he sacrificed the burnt offering himself instead of waiting for Samuel the priest.

Just as Saul was finishing with the burnt offering, Samuel arrived. Saul went out to meet and welcome him. But Samuel was not pleased. "What is this you have done?" Saul replied, "I saw my men scattering from me and you didn't arrive when you said you would." He explained how he felt compelled to offer the burnt offering himself because the Philistines were ready to march against him at Gilgal, and he hadn't yet asked for the Lord's help. "How foolish!" Samuel exclaimed. "You have not kept the command the Lord your God gave you. Had you kept it, the Lord would have established your kingdom over Israel forever. But now your kingdom must end, for the Lord has sought out a man after His own heart. The Lord has already appointed him to be the leader of his people, because you have not kept the Lord's command." (Based on 1 Samuel 8–13.)

It didn't seem that serious. But God has good reasons for His commands. As king, Saul held a position of authority and God was testing his faith. He took Saul to the breaking point and, when he reached the end of his resources, he took matters into his own hands instead of trusting God. He thought he had a good excuse, but Samuel went to the heart of the matter. Saul disobeyed God's command by not waiting for the priest (Deuteronomy 12:5–14). He forgot that God was on his side and would have delivered him, regardless of how serious the circumstances. God's test of faith revealed his true character, and he failed miserably. It wasn't the first time he disobeyed God during his reign. Yet, God made it clear that obedience is more pleasing to Him than sacrifice (Psalm 40:6–8; Jeremiah 7:21–23; Proverbs 21:3). Without a repentant heart and true devotion to God, Saul's sacrifice was nothing more than empty ritual, a substitute for real faith. He lacked the love and commitment to the Lord that leads to obedience. He spent much of his reign in the murderous pursuit of David, his God-appointed replacement, who in stark contrast to Saul, was a man after God's own heart.

God may not have given you an entire kingdom, but He has given you talents and abilities and a means to provide for your daily needs. Like Saul, the pressures of life can test you and reveal your true spiritual character. How do you react in times of adversity, when resources are slipping away in your home or workplace and God is slow to respond to your immediate crisis? Do you get impatient? Cut corners? Take matters into your own hands? We can be disobedient and still appear to be good Christ followers, attend church services, or perform other religious duties. We can hide behind excuses, but God knows the motives of our heart (Proverbs 16:2). Making sacrifices for God, or doing things for the wrong reasons, can even be a subtle attempt to "buy" His provision while maintaining our independence from Him. In contrast, obedience comes from intimacy and total dependence on Him to meet our needs. When you are devoted to God and you know His truth, you can be obedient regardless of the surrounding pressures. Trust Him with all your heart, and do not depend on your own understanding (Proverbs 3:5). Obedience is better than sacrifice.

Prayer

Search my heart, Lord. Reveal my true motives. Show me where I have allowed my impatience with Your timing to lead to disobedience or substituted empty rituals for real faith. I'm sorry for my excuses and attempts to rationalize when I have taken matters into my own hands. Forgive me when I have tried to earn Your favor and provision through my actions. I know You want my obedience, Lord, not my sacrifice.

Help me to trust You, Lord. I want to live a life fully committed to You and Your purposes, even when the pressures mount. Your timing is always perfect. Help me to be a follower after Your own heart, fully obedient out of my love and devotion to You alone.

The Secret to Answered Prayer

"If you abide in Me, and My words abide in you,
you will ask what you desire, and it shall be done for you."
JOHN 15:7 NKJV

Jill sipped her coffee as she listened attentively to her old college roommate, Lois, across the table at the local coffee shop. They met occasionally to catch up, and things were not going well for Lois. For the last fifteen minutes, she had been pouring out a list of problems in her life, everything from her disobedient teenage son, her inattentive husband, her stressful job, her difficult coworkers, her financial struggles, and her mother-in-law. When Jill caught an opening in the conversation, she said kindly, "I'm so sorry you're struggling, Lois. I'll be praying for you." "Humph," Lois retorted. "You can sure try, but it won't do any good. I already prayed about all of it and God didn't do anything." She shrugged. "It is what it is. I guess I just have to deal with it."

For Lois, God was like a cosmic vending machine in the sky where she could visit occasionally, drop her shopping lists of prayers like coins into the machine, and wait for her wants and desires to instantly come out. How often do we do the same thing? We bring our requests to God in prayer, and when we don't get what we want when we want it, we assume He doesn't hear us; He's mad at us, punishing us, doesn't love us; or the answer is *no*. After a few futile attempts, we become disillusioned and stop praying altogether or we reserve our prayers for life-threatening emergencies.

Jesus gave us the secret to answered prayer. Instead of visiting God once in a while to deliver our shopping list of prayer requests, He instructs us to *abide* in Him. When we abide in Him, and His words abide in us, we will ask for what we desire and *it shall be done*. What does it mean to *abide*? Webster's definition is "to remain or continue" and "to stay or live somewhere." For example, most of us live or dwell full-time in our physical homes. With the exception of work and other activities, we eat, sleep, relax, and do life there. Typically, we don't just visit once in a while. In the same way, Jesus wants us to make our home with Him. He wants to be our fulltime dwelling place, not just someone we visit occasionally when we need something. King David wrote about his deep desire to dwell in the house of the Lord, God's presence, all the days of His life (Psalm 27:4). In the Lord's house, he was certain that God's goodness and unfailing love would pursue him forever (Psalm 23:6).

Jesus gave us a different illustration of what it means to abide or remain in Him when He said that He is the vine and we are the branches (John 15:4). He was referring to a grapevine, a prolific plant that bears many grapes. In His example, true Christ followers are branches that stay attached to Him. They know if they are separated from Jesus the vine, they can do nothing (John 15:5). Likewise, anyone who does not stay attached to Him withers and dies and is gathered into a pile to be burned (John 15:6). Amazing things happen when we stay connected to the vine. We receive His nourishment and power to produce much fruit (John 15:5, 8): fruit such as answered prayer, love for others (John 15:12), and immeasurable joy, regardless of our circumstances (John 15:11); fruit like peace, patience, kindness, goodness, faithfulness, gentleness, self-control, and godly character (Galatians 5:22–24; 2 Peter 1:5–8). The fruit we produce through abiding brings great glory to the Father (John 15:8).

How can you stay attached to the vine? Abiding in the Lord is to know Him, worship Him, communicate with Him, and be constantly aware of His power and presence. Abiding means to pray without ceasing (1 Thessalonians 5:16–18). It doesn't mean you spend all your waking hours on your knees with your head bowed, nor does it mean spending fifteen minutes with God in the morning and forgetting about Him the rest of the day. Begin each day by setting your heart and mind on Christ (Colossians 3:2; Hebrews 12:2), and then talk with Him throughout the day. Pray about everything. Tell Him what you need, and thank Him for all He has done (Philippians 4:6). Someone just cut you off in traffic? Sharp words from a coworker? Upsetting phone call? An unexpected expense? Pray! In the same way, praise and thank Him for all the good things that happen throughout your day. Pray until prayer becomes your instinctive response in all situations, especially when anything or anyone tries to steal your joy and derail your intimacy with God. Pray and you will experience a peace far beyond your human understanding because you live in Christ Jesus (Philippians 4:7).

When prayer and worship become as natural as breathing, a God-consciousness develops that flows out of your dependence on Him. You become constantly aware that He is your true life source. He is always with you and always engaged in your thoughts and actions. You are no longer discouraged by unanswered vending-machine prayers because you have made Christ your home, the place where you abide. You are in such a deep place of intimacy that He knows your every need before you ask. Your heart beats with His and His desires have become yours. You have discovered the secret to answered prayer.

Prayer

Lord, I know sometimes I have treated You like a vending machine. I have presented You with my list of wants and grown discouraged or given up when the answers didn't come. Forgive me, Lord. My soul yearns to dwell in Your house (Psalm 84:2). Knowing You and spending just one day in Your courts is better than a thousand elsewhere (Psalm 84:10)!

Lord, I want my communion with You to be as natural as breathing! Throughout my day, help me to set my mind on You and things above, not on earthly things. Remind me to pray and involve You in all the difficulties I encounter, and to always praise You when things go well. Lord, I seek You with all my heart. Help me be constantly aware of Your power and presence in my life. Help me to abide in You! Make Your desires become mine. I delight in You, Lord. Thank You for giving me the desires of my heart (Psalm 37:4). Thank You for answered prayer.

Just Because

The LORD directs the steps of the godly.
He delights in every detail of their lives.
PSALM 37:23

Company was coming and Joy was getting ready. She loved hosting and wanted her house to feel fresh and welcoming. But after she had her carpets cleaned, she noticed the pathway from the kitchen to the great room looked really worn. A small area rug would work perfectly there, she thought. She even saw in her mind's eye exactly what the rug should look like. Later that week, she was heading home after a full day of running errands, and she stopped at a store along the way that she knew carried area rugs. She only had a few minutes due to an evening engagement, so she ran in and went straight to the rug rack, leaving her husband in the car. She flipped through the rugs on the rack. Nothing. And then she saw it. Set apart from all the rest, a spectacular rug caught her eye. It was her rug, the very rug she saw in her mind. She couldn't believe it. The shop owner measured it for her and it was perfect. She rolled it up, paid for it, and even got a discount.

Joy took the rug home and placed it in the faded area. It was absolutely stunning. It drew all the right colors and accents from both adjoining rooms. Later, she found the same rug on the Internet for six times the price she paid! She was ecstatic! Overwhelmed by God's goodness, she knows the rug was a little kiss from heaven. He orchestrated all of the circumstances, everything from highlighting the worn area on the carpet, showing her she needed a rug, and then leading her to the exact rug she'd envisioned, just to show her how much He loves her.

And He did it "just because." She loves sharing her story of a personal Father who delights in every detail of our lives.

Maybe you grew up believing that God doesn't want to be bothered with little things like rugs and home decor. Many of us think mundane everyday concerns, like where we put our car keys, how heavy the traffic is, where we will park, or what we will serve for Christmas dinner are too trivial for His busy schedule. And if He doesn't care about these insignificant needs, why should He care about frivolous wants like blessing us with the perfect rug? Our churches often perpetuate this belief. Posted prayer lists will often be limited to the sick and hospitalized, people in the military, or those suffering the loss of a loved one. Major life-threatening things. But the truth is, God delights in the insignificant.

One of Elisha's young prophets learned just how much God cares and provides for those who trust Him. Elisha and his students were at the Jordan River cutting down some trees to build a new meeting place. While chopping a tree down, one of his young students lost his iron ax head in the river. "Oh no, my lord!" he cried out in despair to Elisha. "It was borrowed!" Elisha simply threw a stick in the water and the ax head floated to the top of the surface. Relieved, the young man reached out and grabbed it (2 Kings 6:1–6).

Did God really care about the lost ax head, enough to raise it from the bottom of the river to the surface? Did He care about blessing Joy with the perfect rug? Yes! When God said He delights in the details of our lives, He meant it. When we need something, He said we can pray about everything (Philippians 4:6). He didn't say pray about some things or pray about the really important things. Don't limit God to prayers for the big things, like a job or money to pay the bills. You can pray about every little worry or concern on your heart, no matter how insignificant you think it might be. And sometimes, it gives Him great joy just to bless you for no apparent reason, like a loving parent who surprises a child with a gift they know their child will love. Don't be surprised if He gives you a kiss from heaven, just to let you know how much He loves you. He is a loving Father who delights in every detail of your life. He wants to be the God of rugs and ax heads! Why? Just because.

Prayer

Lord, You are such a good, good Father! Sometimes I forget just how much You love to bless me. I know it gives me great joy to surprise a child with a gift I just know they will love. Why should it be any different for You? I am Your child, and You are the perfect Father. You know me better than anyone. You know me better than I know myself. Thank You for being such a personal God and for revealing Your love for me in ways that make me smile.

Lord, thank You for delighting in every detail of my life. Today I bring You the small and insignificant things I never thought You cared about. I give them all to You! Help me to pray for everything I need, no matter how small or unimportant. You are a God of infinite abundance, and You never run out of supply. You are a God of infinite time, and You are never too busy to hear my prayers. Lord, thank You for kisses from heaven. Thank You for blessing me with good gifts. . . just because.

Jehovah-Jireh: Sharon's Story

"You have cancer," said the voice on the other end of the line. The three words suspended in the air in front of her, as if waiting for her to take hold of them. She didn't. "But I just came in for a routine colonoscopy," she argued, as if reasoning with him might somehow change his findings. "I'm sorry, Sharon. We'll need to do some more tests to determine if the tumor is contained or if the cancer has spread, and then. . ." His voice trailed off. She tried desperately to process the three incredulous words that landed like a bomb in the peaceful landscape of her consciousness. During the procedure, he found some tissue he sent to the lab, but she wasn't expecting *this*. "But I feel *fine*! I have no symptoms. . ." she continued to reason. "Are you sure? How can this be?" He responded, but she wasn't listening. She had already jumped ahead in her mind to the shock of her untimely death, how she wasn't ready, and how devastating it would be for her husband and children to lose her. What would she tell them? Who would take care of them? She felt sick, as though someone had kicked her in the stomach. Sheer terror grabbed her by the throat and she couldn't breathe. *Calm, I must be calm.* She found her voice, and they finished the conversation. Numb, she wrote down some phone numbers and instructions for the next tests and appointments.

After she gathered herself, she called her husband. He was a calm voice in the midst of the storm. He was also a cancer survivor. He knew. He came home and sat with her, holding her close. Then they headed for church to meet with one of their pastors. She, too, was a cancer survivor.

As they prayed together, she could feel her peace returning. *Thank You, Lord.* "He loves you, Sharon. And He is grieving with you. He will walk with you through this journey. He will never leave you," her pastor affirmed. She prayed for Sharon's healing, and she asked God to quiet her fears. By the time Sharon headed into the first round of tests, she felt hopeful again. *Thank You, Lord. All is well.*

Only it wasn't well. It wasn't well at all. The voice on the other end of the line delivered the latest news matter-of-factly. Further tests revealed two suspicious spots—one in her liver and another in her lung. They didn't know if they were malignant. They might not be. But if they were, it meant the cancer had spread. And stage 4 cancer meant the prognosis dimmed considerably. More tests were in order. *No, no, God. Please no.* The sick, familiar feeling in her gut returned as she tumbled into a deep, dark pit of hopelessness and despair.

Church, must get to church. By the time she sat down with her pastor, she was frantic. Tears spilled out as she explained the latest findings. But as they talked and prayed, her hope began to rise again. She must not jump to conclusions and assume the worst-case scenario, claiming unproven facts as truth, her pastor counseled. She must stand on a higher truth; God is always good and faithful to provide, regardless of our circumstances. Wait on Him and trust Him. She could feel her peace returning. *Wait and trust. Wait and trust.*

And she did. She waited for the next round of test results and trusted Him to provide. Whenever she was tempted to doubt His goodness and fear tried to steal her peace, she simply said, "I trust You, Jesus." The first test came back negative. *Praise You, Jesus.* A few days later, the second test. Again, negative. *Thank You, Lord!* Now the doctors knew what they were dealing with. It was colorectal cancer, but it hadn't spread. It was treatable, but treatment would be aggressive and time consuming. Instead of immediate surgery, her doctor recommended chemotherapy to shrink the tumor and eliminate the cancer.

For the next six months, she clung to Jesus like never before, devouring His Word and resting in His presence. Her family, friends, coworkers, and health care providers were amazed at her "positive attitude." But she knew it was simply a reflection of the peace she carried deep within. It was a peace not of this world. Day after day, God gave her the grace and strength to cope with the chemo treatments, side effects, and uncertainties ahead.

Six months passed and it was time for surgery. The doctors would remove any remaining cancer after the chemo treatments. But now she faced the greatest challenge of all. In order to ensure proper healing and restore full function of her intestinal tract, they would create a temporary opening in her abdominal wall to divert and remove body waste—an *iliostomy* they called it. For six more months, her body would rest while she received *more* chemo to make sure no cancer cells lingered anywhere in her body. And then, they would perform a final surgery to restore everything back to normal.

Six *more* months. It might as well have been six years. . . or an eternity for that matter. *Jesus, I just want my life back.* But day after day, God provided. He gave her the strength to endure the additional chemo treatments. He gave her the grace to manage the iliostomy. Not every day was easy. Sometimes she found herself in that same familiar dark pit of despair. She would cry out to God, and He would reach His hand down to pull her up and back into the light. He would remind her she was His beloved child, and He was a good, good Father. Throughout the extended journey, her family, friends, and health care providers continued to marvel at her attitude. Her joy was infectious. She was an inspiration to others facing cancer and routinely shared her story of hope.

Finally, it was over. One full year had passed since she heard those three words that changed her life forever. She celebrated her last chemo treatment, and a few weeks before Christmas, her surgeon re-routed everything back to normal. She was cancer-free and completely healed and restored. She is now a prayer minister at her local church and prays for others facing difficult trials like cancer. She wants them to know the same God who was faithful to her during the darkest time in her life would be faithful to them, too. Because He is Jehovah-Jireh: the God who provides.

Rejoice Anyway!

Even though the fig trees have no blossoms, and there are no grapes on the vines; even though the olive crop fails, and the fields lie empty and barren; even though the flocks die in the fields, and the cattle barns are empty, yet I will rejoice in the LORD! I will be joyful in the God of my salvation.

HABAKKUK 3:17–18

If only I could find a job. . .
If only I had more money. . .
If only that promotion would go through. . .
If only I had a better boss. . .
If only I could get a decent raise. . .
If only I had no debt. . .
If only my workload would lighten up. . .
If only I could find a spouse. . .
If only I could have children. . .
If only my kids could stay out of trouble. . .
If only I could go on vacation. . .
If only I had a bigger house. . .
If only I had more time. . .
If only I had better health. . .
Then I could be happy.

Do you ever feel you are just one "if only" away from true happiness? If only life was perfect. . .except it isn't perfect. Life is filled with circumstances and events we can't control and expectations others can never meet. True happiness does not come when the current problem is resolved because more problems are on the way (John 16:33). When your happiness depends on these external circumstances, your emotions will run the gamut from the highest peaks to the lowest valleys. When everything is going your way, you're on top of the mountain without a care in the world. Then suddenly, without warning, you lose a job or your business goes under. You face a serious health crisis or a devastating loss. People disappoint you and expectations fall short. You find yourself on an emotional roller coaster plunging into the valley of despair until your changing circumstances take you back up the mountain.

But there is another way to happiness, a way you *can* control. The prophet Habakkuk found it when he looked around at a dying world with a broken heart and rejoiced in the Lord anyway. Shortly before Babylon conquered Judah, he could see the violence and corruption in the land, and he knew disaster was coming. He decided his feelings would not be controlled by the likelihood of barren fields and empty barns, but by God's promise to give him strength. He would rejoice in the Lord, even if the fig trees had no blossoms, the vines had no grapes, the olive crops failed, and the flocks died in the fields. He could not control his circumstances or the impending disaster, but he could control his response. He chose to look past his worldly concerns and praise the Lord, even if everything that mattered to him collapsed. He rejoiced because he knew his Lord would give him strength, joy, and ultimate victory, even in the difficult times to come (Habakkuk 3:2–19).

And the difficult times *did* come. The Babylonians stripped the people from their homeland and held them captive for seventy years. But even then, God delivered His message of hope through the prophet Jeremiah. God would care for the people and prosper them in spite of their captivity if they turned their hearts toward Him. He was planning for good and not disaster, to give them a future and a hope, and to end their captivity and restore their fortunes (Jeremiah 29:4–14). Both Habakkuk and Jeremiah knew that happiness is not based on "happenings," but on our relationship with God.

As you wait for your provision to come, you might have a long list of "if onlys." Will you allow these outward circumstances to steal your joy? Or will you rejoice in the Lord anyway? True joy comes when the Holy Spirit controls your life (Galatians 5:22). It doesn't depend on your finances, your health, or any other circumstance. It doesn't depend on whether or not God satisfies every "if only" on your list. It comes from your relationship with Jesus and knowing He loves you, He lives in you, and He holds your future in His hands. It comes from an unshakable hope in God's ultimate gift of salvation. And since He did not spare even His own Son, you can be sure He will give you everything else you need (Romans 8:32). It comes from knowing that *you* are His precious child, and in Him the highest peaks and the lowest valleys are all the same. Let His Spirit fill you so full that no empty barn, no barren field, no amount of poverty or pain can ever steal your joy again. When Christ reigns in your heart, it won't matter what life throws at you. . .you'll rejoice anyway!

Prayer

Lord, only You know my long list of "if onlys." I know my happiness does not depend on the "happenings" in my life. Yet, I still find myself riding on a roller coaster of emotional highs and lows! Lord, I can't control what happens around me, but with Your help, I can control my response. Give me the grace to trust You and rejoice in You, regardless of my circumstances. Because in You, the mountain tops and the valleys are all the same.

Thank You that You have good things planned for me, not disastrous things, but a future and a hope! Lord, I seek You with all my heart. Help me to rejoice in You, even when the fig trees have no blossoms, there are no grapes on the vine, the olive crop fails, the fields lie barren, the cattle barns are empty, and all my "if onlys" come up short. Fill me with Your presence so that circumstances can never steal my joy again.

Never Thirsty Again

Jesus replied, "Anyone who drinks this water will soon become thirsty again. But those who drink the water I give will never be thirsty again. It becomes a fresh, bubbling spring within them, giving them eternal life."
JOHN 4:13–14

The noon sun beat down on her as she made her way to the well on the outskirts of the Samaritan village of Sychar. She adjusted the clay jug on her shoulder, thinking how heavy it would be when it was filled with water. She sighed. All the other women came to draw water in the early morning and evening when it was cooler, instead of making this mundane trek in the heat of the day. She quickly put the thought out of her mind. It was too late for her. She didn't want to talk to them anyway, and they certainly didn't want to talk to her. They were well aware of her reputation. It was just easier to avoid them altogether.

As she approached Jacob's well, she immediately saw Him. He was sitting by the well, and He looked weary. A traveler stopping for a rest and a drink, she thought. As she came closer, she could see He was a Jew. Odd. Jews never travel through Samaria. They hated Samaritans and regarded them as an impure race. After the Northern Kingdom fell to the Assyrians, her people had intermarried with foreigners and even set up an alternative center of worship. No, a Jew would avoid Samaria. She kept her head down and avoided eye contact, quickly getting to the task of drawing water. And then He spoke to her. "Please give Me a drink." She froze. Not only was He speaking to a Samaritan, but a Samaritan *woman* in a public place. Pausing for a moment, she looked up into the kindest eyes she had ever seen and said, "You are a Jew, and I am a Samaritan woman. Why are You asking me for a drink?"

The man replied, "If you only knew the gift God has for you and who you are speaking to, you would ask Me, and I would give you living water." Confused, she answered. "But sir, You don't have a rope or a bucket and this well is very deep. Where would You get this living water? And besides, do You think You're greater than our ancestor Jacob, who gave us this well? How can You offer better water than he and his sons and his animals enjoyed?" He replied, "Anyone who drinks this water will soon become thirsty again. But those who drink the water I give will never be thirsty again. It becomes a fresh, bubbling spring within them, giving them eternal life."

She thought about her daily trips to the well in the heat of the day and said, "Please sir, give me this water! Then I'll never be thirsty again, and I won't have to come here to get water." But then He said something that made her uncomfortable. "Go and get your husband." "I don't have a husband," she answered. "You're right!" He said. "You don't have a husband—for you have had five husbands, and you aren't even married to the man you're living with now. You certainly spoke the truth!" How did He know about her private life?

She quickly changed the subject. "Sir, You must be a prophet. Why is it that you Jews insist that Jerusalem is the only place of worship, while we Samaritans claim it is here at Mount Gerizim, where our ancestors worshipped?" The man replied, "Believe me, dear woman, the time is coming when it will no longer matter whether you worship the Father on this mountain or in Jerusalem. For God is Spirit, so those who worship him must worship in spirit and in truth." She thought for a moment. "I know the Messiah is coming—the one who is called Christ. When he comes, he will explain everything to us." And then

He said something that pierced her soul. "I AM the Messiah!" Just then, some men approached, obviously shocked to find Him talking to her. But she had already left her water jar beside the well. She ran back to the village to tell everyone about the man who knew everything she ever did. (Based on John 4:1–29.)

Just as our physical bodies need food and water to sustain life, our souls need spiritual food and water to survive and thrive. When Jesus crossed a cultural barrier to offer this woman pure and fresh water that would quench her spiritual thirst forever, He showed her His offer was for everyone, regardless of race, social status, or past sin. All the years she'd tried to fill the deep longing in her soul with men had left her empty and alone. She knew only the promised Messiah could give this gift of living water that would forever satisfy her soul's desire.

God created each of us with the same void inside, a longing only He can fill. It was part of His design so we would thirst for Him, just as our physical bodies thirst after water. The psalmist compared this deep longing to a deer whose life depends on water (Psalm 42:1–2). Stripped of all his possessions, King David cried out desperately to God in the barren wilderness, "My whole body longs for you in this parched and weary land where there is no water" (Psalm 63:1). Sometimes, we reject His living water and instead dig cracked cisterns for ourselves that leak and hold no water at all (Jeremiah 2:13). We try to satisfy our thirst with worldly things like power, prestige, possessions, social status, and achievements that leave us empty. The Samaritan woman discovered that the water Jesus offered her would satisfy forever.

Beloved, this same offer is for you. God's invitation is free and open to all who thirst (Isaiah 55:1). His Spirit will come on all who drink and rivers of living water will flow from their hearts (John 7:38). Come and drink, and you will never be thirsty again.

Prayer

Lord, You are the fountain of life (Psalm 36:9). Forgive me when I have rejected Your fountain of living water and instead dug cracked cisterns for myself that hold no water at all! Show me where I have tried to fill the void in my soul with everything but You! Lord, You are all I need. Only You can truly satisfy all my wants and desires. Help me to thirst after You like a deer pants for water.

Lord, thank You for the gift of eternal life, the fresh bubbling gift within me that flows from my heart forever. Jesus Messiah, thank You that You are the living water that will forever quench my thirst for God. I come and drink, Lord. I will never be thirsty again.

The Secret of Being Content

I know what it is to be in need, and I know what it is to have plenty.
I have learned the secret of being content in any and every situation,
whether well fed or hungry, whether living in plenty or in want.
Philippians 4:12 niv

Warren led a full life of Christian service. He raised five children in the church, served on the church council, started a ministry for motorcyclists, and led many Bible studies over the years. Nothing really changed for Warren when he was diagnosed with Lou Gehrig's disease (ALS) in his early seventies, except for adapting to the significant mobility, communication, nutrition, and other physical challenges of the condition. He simply traded his motorcycle for an adaptive bicycle and kept on riding. He still joked and laughed with his large family of twenty-three grandchildren and four great-grandchildren. He still attended church and Bible study and enjoyed socializing with his friends. Warren's joy-filled attitude lifted everyone who came in contact with him. Throughout his walk with the Lord, he had learned the secret of being content.

The apostle Paul knew the same secret. All through his life he experienced extreme poverty, abundant wealth, and everything in between, including many fiery trials in his service to Christ. Numerous times during his missionary journeys, he faced angry mobs, dangerous deserts, and stormy seas. He was whipped, beaten, bound in chains, thrown into prison, stoned, shipwrecked, and robbed. He spent many painful and sleepless nights without food, water, or enough clothing to keep him warm (2 Corinthians 11:23–27).

Paul spent the last years of his ministry under house arrest in Rome while awaiting trial. Although his living conditions were not nearly as deplorable as the typical Roman prisons of the time, he was likely chained to a Roman guard twenty-four hours a day. He couldn't travel, plant churches, and do the missionary work God called him to do; his trial was years away, and he had no idea how his ordeal would end. From prison, he wrote many of the Epistles, including a letter to the church in Philippi to thank them for a gift they had sent him and to encourage them in their faith. Paul planted this church on his second missionary journey (Acts 16:11–40), and the Philippians had a special place in his heart. He wanted to make sure they understood how he could be filled with joy, in spite of his circumstances, and how they could experience the same contentment.

Paul's secret was to know Christ and experience His power. In fact, he counted everything else as garbage when compared to his relationship with the risen Lord (Philippians 3:8–10). Knowing Christ was his ultimate goal and his top priority in life, above even his family, friendships, and freedom. From this deep place of intimacy, Paul could see his circumstances from God's perspective. He was able to focus on what God called him to do and trust in His promise to supply all his needs (Philippians 4:19). He could draw on Christ's power to give him strength in any situation (Philippians 4:13). He could detach himself from the nonessentials and live *above* his circumstances by focusing on the eternal (Philippians 4:8). Through his own personal experience, Paul could encourage his dear friends at Philippi: "Always be full of joy in the Lord. I say it again— rejoice!" (Philippians 4:4).

Are you struggling to be content and find joy in your current circumstances? Often, our discontentment arises from a true need for our circumstances to change. Sometimes it comes from a realization that they never will. And sometimes, we are drawn to something we think we need to satisfy the emptiness inside—an emptiness only God can fill. Whatever the reason for your discontent, God is bigger and He is enough. He was bigger than Paul's imprisonment and Warren's ALS, and He is bigger than any situation you face today. Take your challenge to God and ask Him to show you His perspective. In His strength, you can rise above your circumstances. Shift your focus away from whatever you lack or whatever is stealing your joy, and focus instead on God and the things of heaven (Colossians 3:2). When you fix your thoughts on what is true, honorable, right, pure, lovely, admirable, and worthy of praise (Philippians 4:8), your circumstances will shrink before your very eyes and lose their power over you. A profound serenity and peace will come, and you will be full of joy in the Lord, a joy that no circumstance can ever steal from you. You may know what it is to be in need, but you have learned the secret of being content.

Prayer

Lord, I may not have experienced all of Paul's fiery trials, but You know I've had my share. Regardless of my situation, whether I am in need or I have plenty, I want to have the same contentment Paul had. I want to know You, Lord. Help me put my relationship with You first in my life. I want to draw on Your power for strength in any circumstance. I want to be full of joy in the Lord!

Lord, forgive me when I try to satisfy the emptiness inside of me with a want or desire other than You. I'm sorry when I focus on what I lack instead of all I have. I have You, Lord, and You are bigger than any challenge I face today. Help me see from Your perspective. Pull me up above my circumstances and help me fix my eyes on things of heaven. Thank You, Lord. My contentment is in You alone.

All You Need

Each time he said, "My grace is all you need. My power works best in weakness." So now I am glad to boast about my weaknesses, so that the power of Christ can work through me.

2 CORINTHIANS 12:9

Late in her career, Ellen became a pastor. It surprised the people closest to her that she would choose such a profession. She was never known to be compassionate and sympathetic. Some would even call her "tough," especially her children. She was not a passive mom. She set the boundaries and expected them to follow the rules, or else. In business, she was a strong, accomplished leader. She was a thinker, efficient with her time, spoke her mind, and didn't wilt when someone disagreed with her. Some found her confidence and intellect intimidating. But in her pastoral role, everything changed. With her natural strengths set aside, she had a deep love and compassion for hurting people, especially those facing a life-threatening health crisis, unspeakable trauma, or the loss of a loved one. She could enter their human pain in a way that many find uncomfortable or avoid all together. She wept with them, prayed with them, and listened as they shared their broken hearts. She didn't choose her ministry. God chose her. He knew her strengths and her weaknesses. And He knew the place where His power would work best.

God's power clearly worked through the apostle Paul. As a gifted self-reliant, highly esteemed Jewish leader, he could have stayed in the comforts of home, enjoying the company of priests and kings and the status of his high-ranking position as a Pharisee. Instead, he found himself crushed, overwhelmed, and fully expecting to die. As if the fiery trials he faced weren't difficult enough, Paul was afflicted with a thorn in his flesh that some scholars thought was some sort of debilitating physical ailment. He asked the Lord to remove it three times, and three times the Lord said no: "My grace is all you need. My power works best in weakness" (2 Corinthians 12:7–10). This ailment was a hindrance to his ministry, but Paul performed extraordinary miracles in spite of it. His suffering kept him humble and made him depend on God instead of his own skills and abilities.

Paul learned he could do nothing without God's grace. The Lord's power alone delivered him from mortal danger (2 Corinthians 1:8–10). He counted all his impressive human abilities, achievements, and credentials as worthless garbage compared with the greatness of knowing Christ (Philippians 3:4–8). He knew he could do nothing apart from Him (John 15:5), and he could do all things through His strength (Philippians 4:13). God chose Paul to become the greatest faith hero in history, even though he murdered Christians and scoffed at the name of Christ. He called himself the worst sinner of all, but God showed him mercy. God's grace completely transformed him, filling him with faith and love for Jesus. He never forgot he was once a sinner saved by grace (1 Timothy 1:15–16). The thorn didn't matter. His weakness didn't matter. Paul knew the power of God's grace, and it was all he needed.

God's grace is the power to do whatever it is you need to accomplish. It was never God's plan that you should be weak and ineffective. He gave you gifts and strengths and the power to use them for His glory. But sometimes life puts up roadblocks and setbacks like Paul's thorn that attempt to hold you back.

When unexpected obstacles come, only by His grace can you keep moving forward. Grace gives you the power to do what you could never do on your own.

Sometimes, we have to voluntarily lay down our strengths in order to trust God. Our own abilities and resources can get in the way of God's plans and purposes, and we can become frustrated and even prideful. We realize we're trying to do His work on our own power, and not relying on God. By recognizing our limitations, we affirm our dependence on God and His strength. We choose to place our trust in Him instead of our own energy, efforts, and talents. When God's grace works in our weakness, there is nothing in us blocking His way and no human effort to resist Him. He can freely move in and through us to accomplish His purposes. We can do with ease what we can't do on our own power without struggle and frustration.

Beloved, God chose Ellen, and He chose you. He knows your strengths, and He knows your weaknesses. He knows the places where His power works best. His grace makes you stronger than you could ever be without Him. His grace is all you need.

Prayer

Lord, thank You for the gift of grace! By faith, Your grace saved me from eternal destruction when I couldn't save myself (Ephesians 2:8). By Your grace, I can accomplish Your eternal plans and purposes for my life, the things I could never do on my own. Your grace made me a new creation and completely transformed my life. Thank You for filling me with faith and love for Your Son.

Thank You, Lord, that Your power works best in my weakness. Forgive me when I have depended on my own energy, efforts, and talents instead of You and Your grace. Help me to lay down my strengths in order to trust You. I want to get out of Your way so Your power can work in and through me. To you alone be the glory. Your grace is all I need.

The Lord Will Provide

And Abraham called the name of that place Jehovah-jireh:
as it is said to this day, In the mount of Jehovah it shall be provided.
GENESIS 22:14 ASV

This book began on the top of Mount Moriah where Abraham was ready to sacrifice his long-awaited son Isaac. When God saw the extent of his faithfulness and obedience, He provided a ram for the sacrifice instead of the boy. Abraham appropriately named the place Jehovah-Jireh, meaning "the Lord will provide." Two thousand years later on that same mountain, God sacrificed His own Son, the Lamb who would take away the sins of the entire world. The Lamb of God first entered the world as a humble baby, born to a virgin girl in a lowly stable in Bethlehem. A son of a carpenter and oldest in a large family, He grew up in height and in wisdom, and He was loved by God and by all who knew Him (Luke 2:52). Finally, at the age of thirty, He launched His public ministry. "The Kingdom of God is near!" He began preaching throughout Galilee. "Repent of your sins and believe the Good News!" (Mark 1:15). He wanted people to understand that the coming of God's Kingdom changed everything.

On another mountain, a mountain near Capernaum, He taught His disciples and a large crowd of followers about this Kingdom (Matthew 5:1–2). In what would become known throughout history as the Sermon on the Mount, He assured them they would be blessed. But blessing in His Kingdom would be different from the familiar values of the world and those of the religious leaders of their time. The world's values of wealth, power, and position are temporary and focus on external circumstances, while Kingdom values are eternal and focus on faithful obedience from the heart. The Kingdom gives when the world takes, loves when the world hates, and helps when the world abuses. He taught them these Kingdom values in the form of eight blessings that His true followers receive through God's grace. These blessings, called Beatitudes, were declarations by Jesus about who we are becoming as children of God, the enviable characteristics we take on as we come to know Him and grow in our relationship with Him.

A closer look reveals how each blessing guides you today as you seek God's provision in your daily life and work. For example, when Jesus taught, "God blesses those who are poor and realize their need for him, for the Kingdom of Heaven is theirs" (Matthew 5:3), He reminds us that we do nothing on our own power, and we need Him to accomplish our purposes. The world may value pride and independence, but true success comes from humility and dependence on God (Isaiah 57:15; James 4:6, 10).

When He taught, "God blesses those who mourn, for they will be comforted" (Matthew 5:4), He wants our hearts to break when we encounter evil in the world and in our workplaces, and for us to recognize and apologize when we ourselves have taken advantage of others to achieve success. The world may value happiness at any cost, but the Kingdom values repentance and compassion (Psalm 51; James 4:8–9).

When He said, "God blesses those who are humble, for they will inherit the whole earth" (Matthew 5:5), Jesus is teaching us the importance of being a servant leader and to use our gifts and talents to lift others up. The world may value power and reward those who are arrogant and self-promoting, but the Kingdom blesses those with a servant's heart (Psalm

37:7–11; John 13:12–15).

When Jesus taught, "God blesses those who hunger and thirst for justice, for they will be satisfied" (Matthew 5:6), He reminds us to keep a right relationship with Him as well as our family, coworkers, and community, and to work against injustice to set the wrong things around us right. The world may reward the pursuit of personal gain at others' expense, but the Kingdom values righteousness (Isaiah 11:4, 5; John 16:8).

When He said, "God blesses those who are merciful, for they will be shown mercy" (Matthew 5:7), He is teaching us to treat people better than they deserve and forgive those who have wronged us just as He has forgiven us. The world may value toughness, but God blesses those who remember the mercy He has shown them and extend it to others (Psalm 25:6–7; Ephesians 5:1–2).

When He taught that "God blesses those whose hearts are pure, for they will see God" (Matthew 5:8), He is reminding us of the importance of integrity and undivided loyalty to Him in our thoughts, words, and actions. The world may overlook deception and dishonesty, but in the Kingdom, knowing our identity in Christ causes us to do the right thing even when no one is looking (Psalm 24:3–5; 1 John 3:1–3).

When He said, "God blesses those who work for peace, for they will be called the children of God" (Matthew 5:9), He is teaching us to make peace in our homes, workplaces, and communities. The world may react to conflict through threats, intimidation, force, or passivity, but true peace comes from relationships founded on godly love and trust (Isaiah 60:17; Romans 12:9–21).

And finally, in the last Beatitude, Jesus taught "God blesses those who are persecuted for doing right, for the Kingdom of

Heaven is theirs" (Matthew 5:10). He reminds us that we are living and working in a fallen world that will always oppose us when we stand up for Kingdom values. But we can take hope in knowing a great heavenly reward awaits us, and He will provide everything we need to finish the race (2 Timothy 3:12; Hebrews 11:39; 12:1–2).

Three years after this infamous sermon, the Lamb of God died on Mount Moriah. But through His resurrection, His Kingdom lives forever (Luke 1:33). He didn't just die to give you eternal life in the future; He died to give you abundant life today (John 10:10). Life in His Kingdom began the moment you came to know the only true God and Jesus Christ, the one He sent to earth (John 17:3). There will come a time in the future when God will reign forever over His perfect Kingdom (Micah 4:2; Revelation 21:10–14). But until then, Jesus made His Kingdom available today. On the mountain of the Lord, you can live the life of blessing you were created to live. You don't have to live according to the world's values, striving to get ahead, accumulating wealth and power, and chasing empty promises that will never satisfy. No, you are entitled to every spiritual blessing in the heavenly realm because *you* are a citizen of His Kingdom (Ephesians 1:3; 2:19). You are a child of God, and everything He has belongs to you (Galatians 4:7). On the mountain of the Lord, it *will* be provided. So come to the mountain and receive all you need (Philippians 4:19). He is Jehovah-Jireh, the God who provides.

Prayer

Lord, thank You for providing the ultimate sacrifice, the Lamb who took away the sins of the world! Lord, when You brought Your Kingdom to earth, You turned the world upside down! Thank You for eternal life in the future and the abundant life I can live right now.

Lord, by Your grace, I am a citizen of Your Kingdom, and I am becoming more and more like You every day. I want more, Lord! I want to know You, the one true God, and carry Your Kingdom values into my home, my workplace, and my community. I come to the mountain, Lord. Thank You, Jehovah-Jireh, for providing everything I truly need.

Jehovah-Jireh: Your Story

The pit is dark and the floor is damp. You no longer see light coming through the opening above. You sigh deeply and wonder, *How did I get here?* There are so many problems—big problems with no solutions in sight. So much need and so much lack—never enough time, never enough money, never enough patience, never enough *you*. Today you have reached the end of yourself. You are empty. You cry out to Him from the depths of your need: "'Rescue me quickly. Have mercy on me, Lord, for I am in distress. Tears blur my eyes. Don't let me be disgraced, O LORD, for I call out to you for help' (Psalm 31:2, 9, 17). I surrender all to Your control. Forgive me for trying so hard to make things work without You."

A few moments of silence pass. And then you see the light. Instinctively, you know He heard your cries. As He reaches out His nail-pierced hand through the opening above, you hear His voice penetrate the darkness below: "Beloved, arise from sorrow, doubt, and depression! Arise from hunger, poverty, and limitation! Arise from confusion, worry, fear, and brokenness! Arise! Shine! Your light has come! My glory has risen upon you!" (see Isaiah 60:1). You grab hold of His hand, and He pulls you out of the pit, setting your feet on the solid ground above (Psalm 40:1). You blink as your eyes adjust to the light. And then you gaze into the kindest face you have ever seen—the face of love itself.

He smiles. "Walk with Me," He says. "I want to show you some things you do not know" (see Jeremiah 33:3). Again, He reaches out His hand, and without saying a word, you take it and begin walking with Him. Wildflowers, ferns, and deep green foliage line each side of the path as it meanders through a wooded sanctuary. The air is crisp and clean, and dappled sunlight dances through the canopy of trees above. You hear the gentle sound of running water nearby. The beauty is surreal. For a while you walk in silence, and then He asks, "Beloved, do your current problems change My love for you?" He pauses and answers for you. "No, neither death nor life, neither angels nor demons, neither the present nor the future, nor any powers, neither height nor depth, nor anything else in all creation, will be able to separate you from My love" (see Romans 8:35, 37–39). You ponder the truth of His words.

As you continue to walk together, the sound of running water draws closer. He leads you down a narrow path toward a deeply wooded area. As you draw closer, you see a cavern in the hillside sheltered by beautiful foliage. He leads you inside, and the sight and sound take your breath away. A wall of water pours down gently from the small cliff above into a beautiful pool below, leaving gentle ripples in its wake. He sits down on one of the large rocks surrounding the pool. He points to another one and motions you to sit next to Him.

Gesturing upward, He says, "Beloved, My unfailing love is as vast as the heavens, and My faithfulness reaches beyond the clouds. My righteousness is like the mighty mountains and my justice like the ocean depths." He pauses and looks deep into your eyes. "You are My child and I created you. I care for My creation, people and animals alike. All humanity finds shelter in the shadow of My wings." Nodding toward the wall of water, He continues, "I feed them from the abundance of My own house, letting them drink from My river of delights. For I am the fountain of life, the light by which you see" (see Psalm 36:5–9).

His words penetrate the depths of your soul. *And I would doubt His care for me?*

He pauses while the sound of the falling water fills the silence. And then He says, "Even strong young lions sometimes go hungry, but those who trust in [Me] will lack no good thing (Psalm 34:9–10). [They] will live safely in the land and prosper" (Psalm 37:3–4, 11). You ponder your current circumstances. Somehow, He knows. "Even in hard times, you will have more than enough," He says gently (see Psalm 37:19). "Make Me your hope and confidence, and you can be like a tree planted along a riverbank with roots reaching deep into the water, not bothered by the heat or worried by long months of drought. These trees bear fruit in every season. You, too, can bear fruit in every circumstance of life and prosper in all you do" (see Psalm 1:2–3; Jeremiah 17: 7–8).

Again, He waits for you to process His words. "Beloved, you know My promise of provision—seek My Kingdom first, and I will give you everything you need (see Matthew 6:33). Yet, you struggle still with doubts and *what ifs*." He stands up. "Come. There is more I want to show you." You are barely on your feet, when suddenly, you find yourself in another place (Revelation 4:2). You gasp at your surroundings, trying to take it all in. Human words can't describe it. There is no ceiling and no floor, yet you are standing firm before a magnificent door covered in shimmering gold with ornate carvings, craftsmanship beyond the skill of human hands. You look at Him in wonder, and He smiles back. "Beloved, no eye has seen and no human heart can behold the treasures behind this door" (see 1 Corinthians 2:9). Before you can begin to imagine, He explains, "These are the treasures you have stored in heaven, where moths and rust cannot destroy, and thieves do not break in and steal (see Matthew 6:19–21); treasures you stored when you honored me with your first fruits and brought Me your tithes (see Proverbs 3:9–10; Malachi 3:10); and treasures you stored when you sowed your time and resources into My Kingdom instead of the world, and made sacrifices in My name" (see 2 Corinthians 4:18; Hebrews 12:27; Matthew 19:29).

You can scarcely take it in when He takes your hand again. In an instant, you find yourself in front of a different door, equally as magnificent but covered instead with solid pearl. Confused, your eyes search His. "I supply all your needs from the glorious riches behind this door" (see Philippians 4:19). And then He says gently, "Beloved, there are blessings in this storehouse you haven't yet asked for, blessings you haven't trusted Me to provide."

Oh Lord! He sees grave concern on your face and continues: "Sometimes My children don't have because they don't ask, and when they do, they ask for the wrong things or they ask for the wrong reasons (see James 4:2–3). My child, you can come to Me with bold confidence and receive whatever you ask because you obey Me and do the things that please Me (see 1 John 3:21–22). You can come to Me like a child who depends on a loving parent to meet his daily needs and fully expect to receive (see Matthew 7:9–11; 18:3). You can give Me all your worries and cares because I care for you" (see 1 Peter 5:6–7). He smiles again. "Like an earthly parent who delights in surprising a child with a long-awaited gift, I delight in giving you your heart's desires" (see Psalm 37:4).

In awestruck wonder, you drop to your knees and praise Him. You can do nothing else. "I give thanks to the Lord who pours His unfailing love upon me, the God who gives me life (see Psalm 42:8)! In my desperation I prayed, and the LORD listened (Psalm 34:6). He turned to me and heard my cry. He lifted me out of the pit of despair, out of the mud and the mire. He set my feet on solid ground and steadied me as I walked along. He has given me a new song to sing, a hymn of praise to [my] God (Psalm 40:1–3). Lord, I sing Your praises and I will not be silent. I will praise You forever (see Psalm 30:12)! To You who opens the floodgates of heaven and pours out Your blessing until it overflows, to You be the glory forever and ever (see Malachi 3:10)! To You, Jehovah-Jireh, the God who provides!"

About the Author

Mary J. Nelson is an author, speaker, and deployed pastor of prayer at Hosanna!, a church of seven thousand members in Minneapolis-St. Paul, Minnesota. She has a passion for helping people know God and His goodness and be empowered and set free to live out their destiny. She is the author of *Grace for Each Hour: Through the Breast Cancer Journey* (Bethany House, 2005), *Hope for Tough Times* (Revell, 2009), and *Peace for Each Hour* (Comfort Publishing, 2013). Her latest books, *Jehovah-Rapha: The God Who Heals* and *Praying for the Cure: A Powerful Prayer Guide for Comfort and Healing from Cancer*, were both released by Shiloh Run Press in 2016. Her books inspire those suffering from physical, emotional, relational, and spiritual brokenness and other life challenges to seek God's heart. She serves on the International Healing Institute's guest faculty and founded and leads the Pray for the Cure cancer healing and discipleship ministry at Hosanna! where she also serves in the Sozo inner healing and healing prayer ministries. She and her husband, Howie, have two adult children and two grandchildren and have been married for 40 years.

If You Liked This Book, You'll Also Like. . .

Jehova-Rapha: The God Who Heals
by Mary J. Nelson

Jehovah-Rapha: The God Who Heals features 72 comforting and encouraging meditations and stories based on healing scriptures—pointing readers to God, the Ultimate Healer. Written by author, speaker, pastor of prayer, and cancer survivor, Mary J. Nelson shares the Word without compromise, releases hope, and focuses on the heavenly Father's infinite love and grace.
Paperback / 978-1-63409-198-5 / $14.99

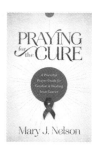

Praying for the Cure
by Mary J. Nelson

This powerful guide offers a closer relationship with the Ultimate Healer. Prayer opens worlds of possibilities—but many people still struggle to pray. *Praying for the Cure* will help readers pray, by offering solid biblical reasons to talk to God and includes specific prayer starters for men and women living with cancer.
Paperback / 978-1-63409-201-2 / $14.99